Punk R

Simon Stephens' play *Bluebird* was produced by the Royal Court in London in 1998. He was Pearson Writer-in-Residence at the Royal Exchange Theatre in 2000–1, and the Arts Council Resident Dramatist in 2000 at the Royal Court. His next play, *Herons* (Royal Court, 2001), was nominated for the Olivier Award for Most Promising Playwright. His radio play *Five Letters to Elizabeth* was broadcast on BBC Radio 4 in 2001, and *Digging* on BBC Radio 4 in 2003. His next stage play, *Port* (Royal Exchange, Manchester, 2002), was awarded the Pearson Award for Best New Play in 2001–2. *One Minute* was produced by the Actors' Touring Company, Sheffield, in June 2003; *Christmas* premiered at the Pavilion Theatre, Brighton, in the same year. Both plays transferred to the Bush Theatre, London, in 2004. *Country Music* was produced by the Royal Court in 2004. Subsequent plays include *On the Shore of the Wide World* (Royal Exchange and National Theatre, 2005; awarded Olivier Best Play, 2005); *Motortown* (Royal Court, 2006; awarded the *Theater Heute* award for Best Foreign Playwright, 2007); *Pornography* (Deutsches Schauspielhaus, Hannover, 2007, invited to the Berlin Theatertreffen, 2008); and *Harper Regan* (National Theatre, 2008). He is currently Artistic Associate at the Lyric Hammersmith.

Simon Stephens

Punk Rock

Methuen Drama

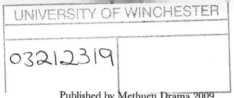
Published by Methuen Drama 2009

5 7 9 10 8 6 4

Methuen Drama
A & C Black Publishers Limited
36 Soho Square
London W1D 3QY
www.methuendrama.com

ISBN: 978 1 408 12636 3

A CIP catalogue record for this book is available from the British Library

Typeset by Country Setting, Kingsdown, Kent
Printed and bound in Great Britain by
Good News Press, Ongar, Essex

Punk Rock

*This play is written for Chris Reeves and Peter Nuttall.
With massive thanks to James Siddely, who taught me
General Studies and told me when I was seventeen
that I could be a writer if I wanted to.*

Punk Rock was first presented at the Lyric Hammersmith on 3 September 2009 in a co-production between the Lyric Hammersmith and the Royal Exchange Theatre, Manchester. The cast, in order of appearance, was as follows:

William Carlisle	Tom Sturridge
Bennett Francis	Henry Lloyd-Hughes
Chadwick Meade	Harry McEntire
Lilly Cahill	Jessica Raine
Cissy Franks	Sophie Wu
Nicholas Chatman	Nicholas Banks
Tanya Gleason	Katie West
Lucy Francis	Ghazalah Golpira
Dr Richard Harvey	Simon Wolfe

Director Sarah Frankcom
Designer Paul Wills
Lighting Designer Philip Gladwell
Sound Designer Pete Rice

Characters

William Carlisle
Lilly Cahill
Bennett Francis
Cissy Franks
Nicholas Chatman
Tanya Gleason
Chadwick Meade
Lucy Francis
Dr Richard Harvey

The play is set in the present day.

The first six scenes of the play are set in the library of the Sixth Form of a fee-paying grammar school in Stockport.

The seventh scene is set in Suttons Manor Hospital.

Scene One

'Kerosene' by Big Black.

It's Monday 6 October, 8.31 a.m.

Lilly Cahill *and* **William Carlisle** *are alone in the library.*

William   When did you arrive?

Lilly   Last week.

William   Whereabouts are you living?

Lilly   In Heaton Moor.

William   Whereabouts in Heaton Moor?

Lilly   At the top of Broadstone Road. By the nursery there.

William   That's a nice street.

Lilly   I think so.

William   Which number's your house?

Lilly   23.

William   23. Right. The houses on that street are some of the oldest in Stockport, did you know that?

Lilly   No.

William   They're old nineteenth-century industrialist houses. Some of the shops on Heaton Moor Road are even older. Practically medieval. Is it very different here?

Lilly   It is a bit.

William   Have you settled in yet?

Lilly   I don't know.

William   It must be slightly disorientating having to adjust to a new town in such a short space of time, is it?

Lilly   It's not too bad. I'm used to moving about.

William   Why?

Lilly   My dad's worked in four different universities in the past twelve years. I've grown immune to it.

William   Was Cambridge the best?

Lilly   Not really.

William   Were the people there unthinkably intelligent?

Lilly   No. They were rude, horrible pigs.

William   Did they have enormous foreheads and big bulging brains?

Lilly   No. They were really rich and stupid.

William   I want to go to Cambridge.

Lilly   Do you?

William   That or Oxford. It's my life's ambition. How did you get here?

Lilly   What?

William   What mode of transport did you use? To get to Stockport, I mean. Not to school. Although you can tell me what mode of transport you used to get to school if you'd prefer.

Lilly   We drove.

William   With everything packed in the car or did you hire a removal company?

Lilly   We hired a removal company. We had some things packed in the car.

William   I like your haircut.

Lilly   Thanks.

William   Is that coat real fur?

Lilly   No.

William   It's *faux*?

Lilly   That's right.

William   That's a relief.

Lilly   Yeah.

William   It'd be terrible if you were some kind of animal killer. Imagine my embarrassment.

Lilly   I'm not.

William   The fur trade's abominable. People who wear fur coats should be skinned alive in my opinion.

Lilly   Mine too.

William   Good. I'm glad. I'm William.

Lilly   Hi William.

William   I've been coming here for five years. I know the place completely inside out. I know every nook and cranny and everything so, if you want any help . . .

Lilly   Great.

William   I know parts of this school that other people don't even know exist. There are secret corridors. Deserted book cupboards. Cellars. Attics. All kinds of things. You want to know about them? Just ask me. This is the Upper School library. Don't you love it?

Lilly   It's –

William   It's completely hermetically sealed from the rest of the school. They tell us it's to keep the Lower School away. I think it's to keep us contained. Look outside.

Lilly   Where?

William   That track leads up to Manchester in that direction and all the way down to London in that direction. The trains come past here all the time. They need to keep us locked in in case we escape.

Most of the Sixth Form can't be bothered to come up here any more. They go to the common room. Or to the main library. They spend hour after hour after hour on the internet there. Or rifling through the DVD section. I prefer it here. It's intimate. People don't like books any more. I do. There's a second edition of Walter Scott's *Waverley* from 1817 on the higher stack. You need permission to see it. I could sort that out for you easily by the way, if you'd like me to. Have you got a locker yet?

Lilly   No.

William   You'll need to speak to Edwards. Edwards is all right. His nose is a slightly odd shape, which I've never trusted. I can speak to him for you if you'd like me to. Do you know where to go to eat?

Lilly   I was going to go to the canteen.

William   Don't. You mustn't. Nobody goes there. You'll die very quickly if you start eating your lunches there.

She breaks into a smile.

I'm being serious.

Bennet Francis *and* **Cissy Franks** *enter.*

Bennett   And this monkey is stood on the bus yelling at all the little Year-Seven babies about how he'd stopped smoking and so anybody who smoked that day was getting glassed before they got off the bus. I looked at him. Pulled three cigarettes out. Lit them all at once. Smoked them.

Cissy   All in one go?

Bennett   Oh yes.

Cissy   Didn't that hurt?

Bennett   Viciously.

Cissy   It doesn't look as though he glassed you.

Bennett   Of course he didn't glass me. He likes my arse too much. How was the rest of your evening?

Cissy   It passed.

Bennett   How was your dad?

Cissy   You know. The same. I wish you'd stayed.

Bennett   Yes.

He notices **Lilly***.*

Bennett   Who the fuck are you?

William   Bennett, this is Lilly Cahill.

Bennett   Is it?

William   She's new.

Bennett   Are you?

William   This morning.

Cissy   Is she?

Pause. They look at her. **William** *awaits their verdict.*

Bennett   Did we hear about you?

Lilly   I've no idea.

William   There was a letter.

Bennett   I bet there was. There's always a letter. I'm Bennett.

Lilly   Hello, Bennett.

Bennett   Cahill's a very good name.

Lilly   Is it?

Bennett   It's Irish. From County Galway. It's ancient.

Lilly   Right.

Cissy   I'm Cissy.

Lilly   Hello.

William   Cissy's Bennett's girlfriend.

Lilly   Great.

Cissy   You're not from round here are you?

William   She's from Cambridge.

Cissy   I can tell. From your accent.

Bennett   She's shatteringly astute like that.

William   Yeah. You have to get up really fucking early in the morning to catch her out.

Beat.

Bennett   How long are you here for?

Lilly   I don't know. Until the exams, I think.

Bennett   Brilliant.

Cissy   What are you taking?

Lilly   Geography, History, French and English.

Bennett   Four A levels?

William   She's incredibly clever.

Cissy   Clearly.

Lilly   And General Studies.

Bennett   Yes. Everybody takes General Studies. Nobody goes. Ever.

William   I do.

Bennett   What's Cambridge like?

William   You should too. It's Mr Lloyd. He's great.

Lilly   I hated it.

Cissy   That's good.

Lilly   Why?

Cissy   I only really trust people who hate their home towns.

William   Me too.

Cissy   How are you this morning, William Carlisle?

William   I'm fantastically fucking brilliant, thank you very much for asking. How are you, Cissy?

Cissy   Great. Happy to be here. Happy as a song lark.

William   Good weekend?

Cissy   Thrilling. We had a dinner party on Saturday night. Bennett cooked a salmon. My mother swooned. How was yours?

William   Terrible. Far, far better here.

Nicholas Chatman *enters. He is drinking a protein drink.*

Lilly   Why was it terrible?

Bennett   Shit. I've forgotten everything.

William   What?

Nicholas   You'll never believe what I saw on Sunday.

Lilly   Why was your weekend terrible?

Cissy   What do you mean, you've forgotten everything?

William   You're better off not knowing. Seriously.

Bennett   My English books, my French books, my History books. The works. What did you see?

Nicholas   *One Night in Paris.*

Bennett   Bless.

Cissy   What are you going to do without your books?

Bennett   Lie. Busk it. Copy yours. Steal theirs. I've not seen that film in years and years and years.

Cissy   I've never seen it.

Nicholas   You should do. It's extraordinary.

Lilly   Why?

Nicholas   What?

Lilly   Why's it extraordinary?

William   Lilly, this is Nicholas Chatman. He plays lacrosse. Nicholas, this is Lilly. She's from Cambridge. She's new.

Nicholas *assesses her before he answers her question.*

Nicholas   Right.

Bennett *interrupts him before he's able to.*

Bennett   I like your jacket, Mr Chatman.

Nicholas   Thank you very much, Mr Francis.

Cissy   Can I try it on?

Nicholas   What?

Cissy   Your jacket. Can I? Please.

Bennett   Is it Paul Smith?

Nicholas   Moschino.

Cissy   It's lovely.

Bennett   It looks better on Nicholas.

William   What's your first lesson?

Lilly   Geography. Period 2.

Cissy   Can I keep it?

Nicholas   No. Don't be ridiculous.

William   Who with?

Lilly   Harrison.

William   I've got him, then.

Lilly   What's he like?

Cissy   It smells lovely. It smells all manly.

Tanya Gleason *enters.*

William   He's a little unsettling. He's generally fine.

Tanya *stops and looks at* **Lilly**.

Tanya   Are you Lilly?

Lilly   That's right.

Tanya I'm Tanya.

Lilly Hello.

Tanya Tanya Gleason? MacFarlane asked me to meet you. Did she not say?

Lilly I'm not sure.

Tanya I thought you were going to be in the common room. How did you get up here?

Lilly I just walked.

Tanya She wanted me to look after you today.

Lilly To look after me?

Tanya I've been looking for you for a while.

Lilly I'm sorry.

Tanya We had a letter about you.

Lilly Did you?

Tanya Last Friday. It said you were starting today. That you were coming from Cambridge. That your father was working in the university. That we should be especially nice to you.

Lilly Why did it say that?

Tanya I have no idea. They send us these things. I think they're all a bit dysfunctional. I like your hair.

She smiles. Comes properly into the room.

Lilly My hair?

Tanya It's quite Lilly Allen. I noticed something about Year-Seven kids.

Cissy You noticed something about what?

Tanya About the children in Year Seven.

Cissy When?

Tanya This morning.

Cissy   You're very random sometimes Tanya, sweetheart, I have to say.

Tanya   When they line up. If you push them. They all fall on top of one another. Like little toys.

Cissy   That's really mean. They could break their little bones.

Tanya   We were never as rude as they are. I was terrified of Sixth Formers. I was quite literally frozen with fear. I used to think they threw bricks at you. Flushed your head down the toilet. Set fire to your tie.

Nicholas   Can I ask you a question?

Bennett   I've a feeling you're going to, aren't you?

Nicholas   Have you started revising yet?

Bennett   Are you being serious?

Nicholas   I kind of am, actually.

Bennett   Oh my Lord alive!

Tanya   They're only mocks. You don't need to revise for mocks.

Cissy   I never need to. I never need to revise for anything. I just do the exams.

Bennett   And get 'A's. You tart.

William   It defeats the points of mocks if you revise for them. They're a dipstick of what stage you're at, educationally, at this particular moment intended to help you get a handle on how much revision you need to do from this point onwards as you move towards the final exams.

They look at him for a beat.

Nicholas   Cos I've started.

Bennett   You would have done. Swot.

Nicholas   It's not about being a swot.

Bennett   Yeah it is.

Nicholas   It isn't. It's about wanting to do my best.

Cissy   My mum would kill me if I got less than an 'A' in any subject.

William   Would she literally kill you?

Cissy   Yes. Literally. She'd burn me alive.

Bennett   When do they start, exactly?

Beat.

Cissy   Are you serious?

Bennett   Don't I look it?

Cissy   You don't know when the mocks start?

Bennett   You never believe me about these kinds of things.

Cissy   November 3rd, 8.50 a.m., Main Hall. French. 11.55, Main Hall, Geography. 2.05 p.m., Back Pitch, PE. Finishing Monday 10th, 2.05 p.m, Main Hall, History.

Tanya   You don't do PE.

Bennett   Does anybody?

Tanya   How do you know when the PE exam is when you don't even do PE?

Cissy   I memorised it. I've got a photographic memory.

Nicholas   I like your badge.

A pause.

Lilly   Thank you.

Nicholas   I like the White Stripes . I think they're getting better. Some bands go shit the more they keep going. White Stripes don't. They're fucking great.

Lilly   I think so too.

William   He's only got the last two albums.

Lilly   What?

William   Nicholas. He's only got two White Stripes albums. He only got *Elephant* last term. He's never even heard *White Blood Cells*. Have you?

Nicholas   What?

William   Have you ever even heard *White Blood Cells*?

Nicholas   What are you talking about?

William   See.

Chadwick Meade *enters. He's wearing a new coat.*

Bennett   Holy fucking moly on a horse, it's Kanye West!

Chadwick   Who?

Bennett   Have you ever set fire to a tie, Chadwick?

Chadwick   No.

Bennett   I should think not. With a coat like that who fucking knows what might happen?

William   Chadwick, this is Lilly.

Chadwick   Lilly?

William   Lilly Cahill. She's joining our school. She came from Cambridge. Lilly, this is Chadwick Mead.

Lilly   Hello.

Chadwick   Hello, Lilly. I'm sorry. I wasn't expecting a new girl. It's terribly nice to meet you. Welcome to the school. I hope you are very happy here.

Lilly   Thank you, Chadwick.

Chadwick   Whereabouts in Cambridge are you from?

Lilly   Burwell.

Chadwick   With the castle.

Lilly   That's right.

Chadwick   Built under King Stephen. During the anarchy.
I like Cambridge.

Lilly   Do you?

Chadwick   I prefer it to Oxford. Not only for its beauty,
but I think the university is better. Certainly in its Applied
Mathematics Department. Which is my specialism. My hero
worked at St John's in the twenties. Paul Dirac. Did you ever
hear of him?

Lilly   I didn't I'm afraid.

Bennett   Chadwick, who the fuck ever heard of Paul Dirac?

Chadwick   He predicted the existence of antimatter. He
developed the Dirac Equation which described the behaviour
of electrons. He won the Nobel Prize in 1933. He said, 'The
laws of nature should be expressed in beautiful equations.'
He's fundamental to the way we perceive the world. He was
at Cambridge.

Lilly   I don't know him.

Chadwick   He died in 1984.

William   Nearly ten years before she was born, Chadwick,
you could hardly blame her, pal.

Lilly   Is that really your name, Chadwick?

Chadwick   Yes it is, I'm afraid. It's American in origin.

Tanya   I didn't believe him either, if that's any consolation.
I thought he made it up.

Bennett   I think he made his head up. Who christened you
Chadwick, Chadwick? Which parent?

Chadwick   I wasn't christened. My parents are atheists.

Bennett   I *bet* they're atheists. You'd have to be with a son
like that.

Cissy   With a face like that.

Bennett   Quite. (*He turns to* **Chadwick**.) Stun me.

Chadwick   What?

Bennett   Stun me, Chadwick. Tell me something stunning. Tell me something the like of which I've never even thought possible before.

The others look at **Chadwick**.

Chadwick   Do you know how many galaxies there are in the universe? About a hundred billion. And there are about a hundred billion stars in most given galaxies. That's ten thousand billion, billion stars in the universe. Which works out as about ten million billion planets.

The others look at **Bennett**.

Bennett   It's like having an absurdly clever puppy.

Here. Chadwick.

Chadwick   What?

Bennett   Have a wine gum.

He pulls out a wine gum and pops it in **Chadwick**'s *mouth. He laughs hysterically.* **Chadwick** *takes it out of his mouth. Looks at it. Puts it back in again. Leaves.*

Nicholas   Has anybody seen Copley, by the way?

Cissy   The new teacher?

Nicholas   She's not a teacher.

Bennett   Course she's a fucking teacher. What is she if she's not a teacher? The traffic lady?

Nicholas   She's a student.

Bennett   Yes.

Nicholas   Students don't count. I'm going to ask her out.

Bennett   You should put that on your Personal Statement. 'I am Nicholas Chatman. I am the boy with the biggest horn in the world.'

Tanya   Are you really going to ask a teacher out?

Nicholas   Why not? She's only about six months older than me, I reckon. She came with us to *Macbeth*. She sat next to me. She's having a tortuous time with Year Nine. She kept asking my advice.

Bennett   Nicholas. You're gorgeous. Did you know that? Gorgeous!

William   Are you incredibly nervous about coming to our school?

Lilly   No.

William   You shouldn't be.

Lilly   I'm not.

Cissy   Unless you get frightened of being bored.

Tanya   Yeah.

Cissy   Because it is quite fucking stupefyingly boring.

William   It's not that bad. Don't listen to her. Sometimes it is.

The bell goes.

Cissy   That's my curtain call, suckers.

Bennett   What have you got?

Cissy   Double Maths.

Bennett   You've always got double Maths. I'm not entirely sure it can be good for you.

Cissy *kisses him. He doesn't kiss her back.*

Tanya *stands to leave.*

Cissy   Where are you going?

Tanya   English.

Cissy   A bit early, aren't you?

Tanya   I'm going to see Mr Anderson.

Bennett   Are you going to ask him to impregnate you?

Tanya   What?

Bennett   Cissy told me about your fantasy. Did you hear this, Nicholas? Tanya's biggest dream is to live with Anderson. To be his secret lover. To have his baby. To waddle about his flat barefoot and pregnant. She's absolutely serious about it, by the way.

Tanya   Fuck off.

Bennett   Aren't you?

Tanya   Did you say that to him?

Cissy   I don't believe you, Bennett.

Bennett   It's true. Am I lying? Are you calling me a liar?

Tanya   Cissy. How could – ?

Tanya *goes to say something. Nearly starts crying. Says nothing. Leaves.*

Cissy   Tanya! Tanya, wait!

She follows after her. The rest listen to her calling down the corridor.

Lilly   I need to go and see Mr Eldridge.

William   Do you know where he is?

Lilly   He's in his office. I was there earlier. It's just down the corridor, isn't it?

William   Second left after the common room.

Lilly   That's right.

William   Right then.

Lilly   Good.

William   I'll see you in Geography then, probably.

Lilly   Yes. Probably. Where is that again?

William   J3. Do you know how to get there?

Lilly   I haven't got a clue. If I come back here can I go with you?

William   Of course you can.

Lilly   Are you sure?

William   It would be a pleasure. I don't mind at all.

Lilly   Thanks. Thank you, William. I'll be here at about half past.

William   Perfect. I'll take you the scenic route.

Lilly   Is it always this cold in here?

William   Always. Until they put the heating on. Then it's insufferably hot.

Lilly   I look forward to that.

William   Have fun with Eldridge.

Lilly   I will do. I'll see you in a bit.

William   Yeah. See you in a bit.

Lilly   See you in a bit, Bennett. Nicholas.

Bennett   See you, Lilly Allen.

William   Fuck off, Bennett. Leave her alone.

Lilly *smiles at* **William** *then turns to* **Nicholas**.

Lilly   See you.

Nicholas   Bye.

She leaves.

Some time.

Bennett   'I'll take you the scenic route.'

He and **Nicholas** *giggle at* **William**.

Bennett   Can I ask you something, Mr William Carlisle?

William   Go on.

Bennett   Have you ever actually had a girlfriend before?

William   What are you talking about?

Bennett   Have you?

William   What do you want to know that for?

Bennett   You haven't, have you? I find that quite touching.

William   Piss off, Bennett.

Bennett   You're a bit besotted, mate, aren't you?

She'll break your heart William.

William   I don't know what you're wittering on about.

Bennett *looks at him. Smiles.*

Bennett   No.

Scene Two

'Eric's Trip' by Sonic Youth.

It's Tuesday 14 October, 3.30 p.m.

Lilly *and* **William** *are in the common room.*

Lilly   Do you know what I've noticed about you? You're
very still. You stand very still most of the time. You move your
head quite slowly. I really like it. I like your hair too.

William   Thanks.

Lilly   I like the way it hides your eyes. It looks shy. You've
got shy hair.

William *smiles. Looks away slightly.*

Lilly   How was History?

William   It was unusually dramatic.

We had Lloyd. He was in a peculiar mood.

He came in. We were sitting down. He looked at us for about
three seconds. He sat down. We were all chatting. He looked
at us. We kept chatting. He looked some more. We chatted

some more. He sat still. We chatted. He waited until we
stopped. And then he waited until we were silent. This took
about a minute. And then he just waited. He waited five more
minutes. Said he had decided not to teach us today. He didn't
think we deserved it. Until we said sorry to him. And we did.
One by one. Went round the class. 'Sorry, sir.'

Lilly   Is he your favourite?

William   I think so. I find his classroom-management skills
rather bracing.

Lilly   Have you finished your UCAS form?

William *nods.*

Lilly   Have you sent it off?

William   This morning. Have you?

Lilly   I'm doing it tonight.

William   You better had.

Lilly   Are you applying for a year off?

William   Christ no.

Lilly   Every other fucker is.

William   I can't wait. Just to get out.

Lilly   No. Me neither

She looks at him. Her gaze unnerves him a little.

William   How was French?

Lilly   *Un cauchemar sociologique.*

William   Un whatty-what-what?

Lilly   Do you ever worry about Chadwick Meade?

William   You're losing me.

Lilly   He's in our French lesson. He's a brilliant linguist. He
never says a word. He was rocking for most of the lesson. Ever
so slightly. I was sitting next to him. It really unsettled me.

William   Rocking?

Lilly   To and fro.

William   That sounds rather comforting.

Lilly   It was weird. I'm not entirely sure I trust him. I'm not sure I like him.

William   What's not to like? He's the cleverest man in the universe.

Lilly   He's not normal.

William   I hate normal people. Normal people should be eviscerated. He has a monster of a time. He's on a rather considerable scholarship. His home life is rather ghastly, I think. He has a very difficult time here. You should be nice to him.

Lilly   I hate the word 'should'.

William   The pressure he gets. The thoughts he has. People should be careful around him.

Lilly   That was kind of my point.

William   One day he's going to snap, I think.

Lilly   What do you mean?

William   He's too timid half the time. He should stand up to it. Stick his chin out. I wish he would. I've seen it happen.

Lilly   Seen what happen?

William   People like him who get so much abuse and then one day. Pop.

Lilly   Pop?

William   I like him.

Lilly   I'm glad somebody does.

William   We went to Cambridge University together in the summer holidays. On a visit. He's a lot funnier when you get him on his own. I think he gets nervous of speaking too much in front of people like Bennett. People notice him because of his scholarship tie. He said that it's a constant reminder. He took me to where Isaac Newton studied. He took me to the Botanic Gardens there. Showed me a tree which is apparently a descendent of the apple tree that Newton sat under.

It was unlike anything I've ever seen. Nobody from my family's ever even been to university before. We're not a family where that kind of thing happens.

We went to King's. Which is the college I've applied for. Asked somebody where we should go and look. There was a doctor in there. A scientist. Somebody with, he had a white coat on. He told me we should go and look at the chapel there. He said it was rather beautiful. I'd never heard a man use the word beautiful like that before.

It was beautiful, by the way. Parts of it date from the middle of the fifteenth century. The ceiling is spectacular. It has rather breathtaking fan vaulting. It was designed by Wastell. And built by him, actually.

If my application's accepted I'll have my interview next month. I hope I get one, an interview. They do the mock interviews in here. Lloyd does them. It'd be great. Just me and Lloyd. In here. Having an interview!

It's half three. We should be going home.

Lilly Yeah.

William It's amazing how quickly this whole place empties. I love it. I love being here when it does. You walk down the whole corridor and you're the only one there.

This room becomes like a kind of cocoon.

It's cold today. It feels like it's turning into autumn. I always think you can feel the exact day when that happens in this country.

Can I ask you: how are you getting on?

Lilly What do you mean?

William   Here. How was your first week?

Lilly   It was all right. It was a bit odd. Some of the teachers are a bit strange. It's strange that there are so few of us. It can feel a bit claustrophobic. Bennett does my head in occasionally.

William   What I meant was: what do you think of Stockport?

She thinks.

Lilly   Honestly?

William   Honestly.

Lilly   I've been to worse places. I've lived in worse places. It's not as bad at Plymouth. It's not as bad as Hull. Heaton Moor's nice. We went to Lyme Park at the weekend. It was gorgeous.

William   The deer park there's medieval. If you move slowly enough there are fallow deer there that let you stroke them.

Lilly   The shopping centre in town makes me want to gouge my eyes out, though.

William   Ha!

Lilly   And I hate all the people.

Pause.

William   All of them?

Lilly   Apart from you lot, here.

William   You hate all of the people you've met in Stockport?

Lilly   Yeah.

He looks at her.

William   With their tied-back hair. And their stupid ugly make-up and their burgers?

Lilly   And their faces.

They smile at each other.

William   'What the fuck are you looking at?'

Lilly   'I'm looking at you, you Chav shit.'

William   I know what you mean.

Lilly   Poundstretcher store-card holders, the lot of them.

William   And all the boys are fathers at seventeen and banned from being within a square mile of their children at nineteen and jailed at twenty-one.

Lilly   They deserve it.

William   Because they're thick and they're vicious.

Lilly   And they're fat and they're ugly.

William   And frightened of anything that's different from what they're like.

Lilly   And terrified of intelligence or thought.

William   They're nervous about thinking because if they think too much they might just realise that the way they live their lives with their shell suits and their vicious little ugly little dogs is not necessarily the only way to lead a life.

Lilly   And they can't fucking wait till Christmas. And the furthest they've ever been to is Spain.

William   And even then they hated it.

Lilly   And wanted to eat more egg and chips.

William   Do you know something?

Lilly   What?

William   I always thought I was the only person who thought those kind of thoughts.

Can I tell you: I sometimes think I'm the best person in this town. Is that terrible?

Lilly   No.

William   I'm definitely the cleverest. And the funniest. Don't you think?

She thinks.

Lilly   Yeah.

William   Do you?

Lilly   Yeah.

William   I do too. I think I'm hilarious. Do you ever think about the person you wished you were?

Lilly   Sometimes.

William   When I think of that person, do you know what I realise?

Lilly   What?

William   I realise I *am* him.

Can I ask you? Do Bennett and Nicholas and Cissy ever say anything about me?

Lilly   No.

William   Never?

Lilly   No.

William   Do they never talk about my family?

Lilly   No.

William   Or my job?

Have they told you about my job?

Lilly   What job's that?

Pause. He has to stop himself from chuckling a little, which makes her chuckle a little too.

William   If I told you, you wouldn't believe me.

Lilly   Go on.

William   Nobody believes me.

Lilly   I would.

William   Why?

Lilly   What do you mean?

William   Why would you believe me when nobody else in their right mind would?

Lilly   I'm very trusting.

William   I bet you are.

Lilly   What?

William   I said I bet you are.

He stops chuckling and becomes suddenly serious. She can't stop so quickly.

I work for the government.

Lilly   Do you?

William   See?

Lilly   What?

William   You don't believe me.

Lilly   I never said that. Of course I believe you.

William   Then you're mad.

Lilly   Why?

William   As if a seventeen-year-old would work for the government!

Lilly   You told me you did. I believe you. Even if you try and deny it now, I'll still believe you.

Pause.

William   It's covert.

Lilly   I'm sure.

William   They don't tell anybody about it. People would get freaked out. They'd think I was a bit young.

Lilly   I can imagine. What do you do for them?

William   I observe Muslim teenagers for them. They want to target Muslim teenagers. So obviously they employ a teenager to do it. It would be stupid to employ an adult. So actually they employed me.

Lilly   That sounds exciting.

William   It isn't. Mostly Muslim teenagers are very boring. I have to fill in a brief form every fortnight.

Lilly   Have you cracked any terrorist rings?

William   No. Mainly they play football and snog each other behind their parents' backs.

The two giggle together.

Can I ask you something?

Lilly   Anything.

William   How many hours do you normally sleep?

Lilly   Sorry?

William   On average? Every night?

Lilly   Nine.

William   Nine?

Lilly   Ten sometimes. Eleven if I get an early night.

William   Right.

Lilly   Twelve on a weekend.

William   I sleep four. Can I ask you something else?

Lilly   Of course you can?

William   Don't you ever get frightened?

She looks at him, thinks before she answers.

Lilly   Yes, I do.

He thinks before he presses her.

William   Tell me what kind of things you get frightened of?

She thinks.

Lilly Nuclear war.

Black people.

Dogs. Most dogs. Some birds. Farm animals.

Sexual assault.

I get frightened of waking up in my house and there's somebody there in my room.

Sometimes in the middle of the night when my parents go out my mum storms off. She walks home, comes home early. Really drunk. My bedroom's downstairs. It always is. For the last three houses. I prefer it. She normally forgets her keys so she normally taps on my window to get me to let her in. I sometimes think it's dead people outside. That terrifies me.

William What does she storm off for?

Lilly She gets pissed off at my dad. She drinks two bottles of wine.

William My mum died when I was about four.

I don't really remember her. I never knew my dad. My dad died before I was born.

I don't tell anybody that. That's a secret. Can I trust you to keep that to yourself?

Lilly Of course you can.

William Thanks.

Lilly Do you remember her dying?

William A little bit.

Lilly What do you remember about it?

William I remember the police in our living room drinking tea. The police came round for some reason. I remember one of them had four sugars. I remember her funeral. Everybody patted me a lot.

Lilly   So you're a little orphan boy.

William   That's right.

Lilly   Are you in care?

William   No. I live with my auntie.

Lilly   What's she like?

He smiles. He doesn't answer.

I wouldn't feel too sorry for yourself, by the way.

William   I don't.

Lilly   Parents can be complete shits.

William   I'm sure.

What are those scars? On your arm?

She looks at him before she answers.

Lilly   What do you think they are?

William   Do you cut yourself?

Lilly   You're cute.

William   Do you, Lilly?

Lilly   Watch this.

She pulls out a Bic lighter. She lights it. She keeps it lit for ages until the metal on it is roasting hot. She turns it off. She burns a smiley into her arm with the metal on the top of the lighter.

William   Does that hurt?

Lilly   No. It feels really nice.

He watches her finish it off. She shows it to him.

William   Can I touch it?

She looks at him for a beat. Then she nods.

He does. She winces a bit.

Have you felt how hot I am? Feel my forehead.

She does.

Do you know what I think?

Lilly What do you think, William Carlisle?

William I think our bodies are machines.

He moves away from her. Breaking her touch.

You know where the heat from our body comes from. It comes from the energy it burns up carrying out all of its different activities. That's why corpses are so cold. Because the machine has stopped.

Lilly I'm not a machine. I'm an animal.

William What kind of animal are you?

Lilly A wolf. A leopard. A rhinoceros. A gazelle. A cheetah. An eagle. A snake.

William I feel like I've known you for years.

Lilly You haven't.

William When we were little did we go on holiday together or something like that?

Lilly I don't think so, William.

William I think we did. Did we go camping together?

Lilly No.

William What school did you go to when you were little?

Lilly St Michael's in Tunbridge Wells.

William It can't have been that then.

Would you like to go out with me?

Lilly Go out with you?

William On a date. We could go to the theatre. Or I could take you out for a meal.

Lilly A meal?

William   Even though I hate restaurants.

Lilly   You hate them?

William   They scare the life out of me.

Lilly   Why?

William   All those people watching you eat.

Lilly   Why would you take me there then?

William   We could go to the cinema then. Or bowling. Swimming.

Lilly   Swimming?

William   Have you ever been to Chapel?

Lilly   To where?

William   Chapel-en-le-Frith? It's a village. In Derbyshire. It's somewhere else that's beautiful. We could go next week. In the half term, if you'd like to. We can get a train.

Would you like to?

Would you like to go out with me at all?

Lilly   I don't think so.

A beat.

William   Right.

Lilly   I don't really want to go out with anybody at the moment.

William   Right.

Lilly   It's absolutely not you so don't think that. I just can't be doing with a fucking boyfriend.

William   No.

Lilly   I'm sorry.

Pause.

William   I've never done that before.

Lilly   What?

William   Asked anybody out.

It didn't really go very well, did it?

Lilly   It wasn't –

William   I really fucked it up.

Lilly   No. You did all right.

William   Disappointing outcome though, I have to say.
A complete embarrassment, if the truth be told.

Lilly   I don't think it was. I think it was romantic.

Scene Three

'Loose' by The Stooges

It's Thursday 30 October, 12.46 p.m.

Lilly *and* **Nicholas** *are in the common room.*

Lilly   Hi.

Nicholas   Hi.

Lilly   How's it going in there?

Nicholas   It's going OK. How are you getting on?

Lilly *nods her head at him for a while. Smiles. Says nothing.*

Lilly   How's the revision?

Nicholas   You know.

Lilly   You ready yet?

Nicholas   Oh. I think so.

Lilly   Have you seen William?

Nicholas   Not this morning. Not all day.

Lilly   He's not been in since the break.

Nicholas   I didn't notice.

Lilly   Are you coming out for lunch?

Nicholas   I'm going to the gym.

She looks at him.

Lilly   Come here.

He does.

Take your blazer off.

He does.

Flex your muscles.

He does. She strokes them.

Thank you.

She takes an apple out of her bag. Eats it.

Do you want an apple? I've got a spare one.

Nicholas   I'm all right.

Lilly   He asked me out. William.

Nicholas   When?

Lilly   Before half term.

Nicholas   What did you say?

Lilly   What do you think?

Nicholas   I don't know. Hence me asking.

Lilly   He was really funny. His face went all stupid. I did feel a bit sorry for him.

Nicholas   Why?

Lilly   Have you ever noticed that?

Nicholas   Noticed what?

Lilly   When you think somebody's a complete dick you find out something about them and you can't help feeling sorry for them even if you really don't want to.

Nicholas   What did you find out about William?

Lilly   He told me about his mum.

Has he ever talked to you about her?

Nicholas   Not really. Not much. We're not that close. What did he say about her?

Lilly   She's dead. Did you know that?

His dad died before he was born.

She died when he was little.

He was four. Imagine that.

Nicholas   Did he tell you that, did he?

Lilly   Imagine being four years old and watching your mum die. You have to admit it's a bit heart breaking.

Nicholas   Is that what he said to you? That his parents were dead?

Pause.

Lilly   Aren't they?

Nicholas   When did he say that?

Lilly   Two weeks ago. When he asked me –

They're not, are they?

Nicholas   His dad's an accountant. His mum's a nursery school teacher in Cheadle. She's lovely. She looks really young for a mum. She's quite attractive as it goes.

Lilly   Fuck.

Nicholas   Yeah.

Lilly   That's quite unsettling.

Nicholas   I know.

Lilly   I'm quite unsettled now.

You've unsettled me.

Nicholas   I didn't intend to.

Lilly   Why would he lie about something like that?

Nicholas   I've no idea.

He had a brother. I think this is true. I think he had a brother who died. When he was just a little kid.

Maybe he was −

Lilly   What?

Nicholas   I don't know.

Lilly   Confused? You can't get confused about something like that. You can't mistake one for the other.

He was doing it for attention.

How selfish can you get? I'm tempted to find where he lives and go round and tell them.

Nicholas   Don't.

Lilly   No.

Hey.

Nicholas   Hey.

Lilly   I've been thinking about you all morning. Did you know that?

Nicholas   No.

Lilly   Well, it's true. And I have to say that some of the things I've been thinking are a bit filthy.

He goes to her. Kisses her on the lips.

Nicholas   I've been thinking about you, too.

Lilly   Liar.

Nicholas   Last night.

Lilly   Yeah? What about it?

Some time.

Nicholas   Can I confess something?

Lilly   Go on.

Nicholas   I'd never had sex before.

Lilly   Right.

Nicholas   Could you tell?

What?

What are you laughing at?

Lilly   Men. Boys. They're so . . .

Nicholas   What?

Lilly   Nothing. No. I couldn't tell. I didn't care.

Nicholas   It was fucking amazing.

Lilly   It *was* a bit, wasn't it?

Nicholas   You were fucking amazing.

Lilly   Chump.

Nicholas   Well. It's true.

Lilly.

Lilly   Nicholas.

Nicholas   I don't think we should tell anybody.

Lilly   What?

Nicholas   I think we should keep it to ourselves. That we're going out with one another. I think it'd probably be best if people didn't know.

Lilly   Why?

Nicholas   Don't you think?

Lilly   I don't know.

Nicholas   People here are so −

Lilly   What?

Nicholas   They just go on and on.

Lilly   Are you ashamed of me?

Nicholas   No. Don't be stupid.

Lilly   I'm not being stupid in the least.

Nicholas   I'm not saying that.

Lilly   You just want to keep me as your little secret?

Nicholas   Kind of.

Lilly   Prick.

Nicholas   What?

Lilly   You. You're a prick.

How are things going with Miss Copley?

Nicholas   Are you cross with me?

Lilly   Has she fallen for your overwhelming sexual aura yet, Nicholas?

Nicholas   Have you got the slightest idea what people would say about you?

Lilly   Nicholas Chatman, the Casanova of Nurishment. A million pheromones in every muscle.

Nicholas   Shut up.

Lilly   Honestly, one fuck and he wishes he'd never met me.

Your face!

Nicholas   I'm going.

Lilly   Go and do your work-out. Press those benches, baby. Give them a squeeze from me.

Nicholas   Are you around later?

Lilly   Might be.

Nicholas   Lilly.

Lilly   I'm teasing. I'm sorry. Yes. I'm here later. I'll wait for you.

And OK.

I won't tell anybody.

Nicholas   Thanks. I'm really sorry. I just think. Here.

He kisses her.

I'll see you later.

Lilly   See you later. Arnold Schwarzenegger.

He leaves.

She sits. She looks at her apple. She picks a chunk out of it with her fingers. She eats it. She spits it out after a while.

A train passes outside the window. She looks up to watch it.

Cissy *and* **Tanya** *enter.*

Cissy *is eating a large chip sandwich.*

Cissy   The amount of flour in this bread is fucking ridiculous.

Hi.

Lilly   Hi.

Tanya   Hi.

Lilly   Hi.

Cissy   What do you think these chips are made of?

Tanya   Dough, mainly.

Cissy   I shouldn't be having these. I don't even normally have lunch any more. I just have Skittles. Have you ever had four packets of Skittles in one go? Your brain feels amazing.

The girls smile at this idea. Some time.

Tanya   I think that's really dangerous. Human beings have to eat. It's one of the things that we do. Five pieces of fruit and veg a day. Regulated food groups. Thirty minutes exercise three times a week.

I blame the parents.

The three girls burst out laughing. It takes them a while to recover.

Lilly   Do you ever think about that?

Tanya   Think about what?

Lilly   Being a parent.

Tanya   All the time.

Cissy   She doesn't just mean about having Anderson's children. She means about actually properly being a parent.

Tanya   Yeah.

Lilly   Seriously?

Tanya   Seriously.

A beat.

Lilly   Me too.

Cissy   God.

Lilly   I think I'd be a terrible mother.

Tanya   Don't be silly.

Lilly   My babies would probably all die. Really quickly. I wouldn't know how to feed them. I wouldn't know what to do with them. I'd end up putting them in a cupboard.

Tanya   You wouldn't.

Lilly   I would though.

Cissy   They can't remember anything until they're about five, anyway. You may as well put them in a cupboard. They wouldn't remember you doing it.

Tanya   I'm going to have four.

Cissy   Four?

Tanya   Yep. I'm going to be brilliant. Home educate them. Take them to lots of sports meetings. In my big car.

Cissy   In Anderson's big car.

Tanya   In Anderson's big car.

Lilly   He hasn't got a big car. He comes to school on a bike.

Tanya   Tennis lessons. Football lessons. Ballet lessons. Anything they want. Teach them languages.

Cissy   You don't know any languages.

Tanya   I'd learn. Loads of languages and teach them all to our children.

You've got to admit he's fucking lovely.

Of course he's got a car. He just uses his bike to keep fit. And save the world.

Pause. **Cissy** *eats.* **Lilly** *takes a carrot from her bag and eats that.*

Lilly   Would you have Bennett's children?

Cissy   Fuck. Off.

Lilly   Why not?

Cissy   Can you imagine? They'd be impossible.

They eat for a while.

Lilly   Have you never even talked about it?

Cissy   I think it would scare the shit out of him to even think about mentioning it. He'd pick up on my thoughts.

Lilly *looks at her.*

Lilly   What's he like?

Cissy   What do you mean?

Lilly   Bennett.

Cissy   What do you mean, what's he like?

Lilly   You know.

Cissy   No.

Lilly   In bed.

Cissy   Oh Christ.

Lilly What?

Cissy I'd rather not go into that while I'm having my lunch.

The girls chuckle together. **Lilly** *watches* **Cissy**.

Cissy I'm not going to have children until I'm about forty-two. I'm going to wait until I can afford to pay for somebody else to look after them. I've got too many things I want to do. Too many places I want to go. I can't wait to leave England is one thing. Go and live abroad.

I'm going to. As soon as I finish here.

Lilly Where are you going to go?

Cissy Edinburgh. Glasgow. Dublin. Paris. Anywhere apart from here.

Pause.

She wraps up her sandwich and puts it away. The other girls watch her.

I'm so fat.

Lilly You're not fat.

Cissy Look at me.

Lilly You're not fat. Don't say it because it's not true and it makes it look as if you're really showing off.

Cissy *looks at her. A beat.*

Cissy Yeah.

Another beat. She grins.

What are you girls getting for Christmas?

Bennett *enters.*

Bennett I'm getting really bored of Mahon telling me about gay heroes of literary history. She finds me every day. It's like she waits around corners for me and leaps out.

She makes me summarise articles from the *Guardian* for her.

Cissy It's only because she's too thick to read them herself.

Bennett   She keeps telling me that I could be a lawyer if I wanted to. I don't want to be a lawyer. Who wants to be a fucking lawyer for fucksake?

Tanya   Have you ever thought that there might be a reason?

Bennett   What?

Tanya   That she singles you out for those kinds of suggestions?

Bennett   What the fuck are you implying, Miss Gleason?

Tanya   I'm not implying anything, Mr Francis. I'm just asking a question.

Bennett   Have they put the heating on?

This fucking room.

I need to get outside. I need to go and run around a bit. I need to do PE. I really miss PE. I never thought I'd say that, ever.

Tanya   I don't miss PE teachers.

Bennett   That's because they're fucking retards.

Cissy   Apart from Cheetham.

Bennett   He's a retard. He's a retardus primus.

Cissy   He was very sweet to me.

Bennett   That's because he wanted to finger you.

Cissy   He told me he was really impressed with my GCSE results.

Bennett   Yes, because he wanted to fucking finger you. I told you.

Cissy   Bennett.

Bennett   Would you have let him?

Cissy   Don't.

Bennett   I bet you would. Mind you, I can't say I blame him. People get so het up about inter-generational sexual activity nowadays. It's ridiculous. We should just all jolly well calm down, I think. What's the youngest person you'd fuck, Tanya?

She looks at him. Glances at **Cissy**. *Looks back at him.*

Bennett   Sorry, you go in for the older man, do you not?

Tanya   Are you asking me about *my* sexual experiences, Bennett? That's quite bold coming from you.

Bennett   What does that mean?

She smiles. Says nothing.

I'd finger a Year-Eight girl. If she was up for it. And if she wasn't, I'd definitely have a bit of a posh wank thinking about her.

Cissy   Teachers shouldn't have sex. They're too old. I find it really unnerving. The idea of it. All that old skin. Wobbling about.

Chadwick *enters.*

Bennett   You always used to look forward to PE lessons, didn't you, Chadwick?

Chadwick   What?

Cissy   Do you remember in swimming when he went diving for the brick? You nearly drowned didn't you, sweetheart?

Bennett   Missed opportunity that one, folks.

I remember you in the changing rooms. I remember your little tiny needle dick.

Chadwick.

Tanya   Here we go.

Bennett   Is it true you squeeze lemon juice onto your hair? To make it go blonder?

Chadwick   Sometimes.

Bennett   Does it work?

Chadwick Yes.

Tanya Does it?

Chadwick Yes.

Bennett You're a genius, Chadwick, I think, aren't you?. But you've got to admit –

Chadwick What?

Bennett You look pretty fucking stupid in that coat.

Chadwick Yeah.

Bennett Did you just actually agree with me?

Tanya Shut up, Bennett.

Cissy Some people can wear a coat like that. Some people look like retards.

William *enters. He is frantic. He is drinking a red drink out of a mineral water bottle.*

William Somebody's stolen my money.

They look at him for a beat. He swigs.

Tanya What money?

William I had about a hundred pounds.

Tanya What did you have a hundred pounds for?

William It's not that much.

Lilly Where have you been?

William What?

Lilly You've not been in for days.

William What are you talking about?

Tanya What did you bring a hundred pounds to school for?

William It was in my bag.

Lilly When did you last see it?

William   What do you mean, when did I last see it? What kind of a fucking cunt of a question is that? 'When did you last see it?' This morning. This morning is when I last saw it. I saw it this morning when I put it in there. Somebody's stolen it. People are always doing that to me.

Tanya   Are you sure?

William   Don't I look like I'm sure?

Tanya   I make that kind of mistake all the time.

William   Do I look like a liar?

Tanya   No.

She moves towards him.

He backs away from her suddenly.

William   Were you trying to kiss me?

Tanya   What?

William   Just then?

Tanya   No.

William   Were you?

Tanya   No, I wasn't.

William   'No, I wasn't.' Is that why you moved closer to me?

Tanya   I didn't realise I did.

William   People do that kind of thing though, don't they?

Bennett   William. What are you drinking?

He looks down at his drink.

William   Campari and grapefruit juice.

Do you want to try some?

Bennett   Are you really?

William   Why would I lie about something like that? It's my favourite drink, for goodness' sake. Here.

Bennett *takes it.*

Bennett   Ta.

He drinks.

Wow.

He drinks some more.

Chadwick, have you got any money on you?

Chadwick   I'm sorry?

Bennett   Have you, Chadwick?

Chadwick   What do you mean?

Bennett   I mean have you got any money in your wallet or in your pocket or in your bag or up your arse that you could spare for William? William's lost a hundred pounds and I think you should try and get it back to him, don't you?

Chadwick   It's nothing to do with me.

Bennett   I'm sorry?

Chadwick   I said it's nothing to do with me.

Bennett   Ha!

Chadwick   William, I'm terribly sorry that you've lost some money but I don't really think it was my fault.

Bennett   Chadwick. Get your wallet out.

Tanya   Bennett. Stop it. Now.

Bennett   What? What, Tanya? Are you actually trying to stop me here?

Chadwick, get your wallet out fucking now you fucking cunt-faced twat or I will beat the fucking bricks out of your arse with my bare fists while everybody else watches and sings little fucking songs, so help me God I will.

Chadwick   Here.

Bennett   How much is in there?

Chadwick   Nothing.

Bennett   How much, you lying fuck?

Chadwick   Twenty pounds.

Bennett   Take it out.

Chadwick   What?

Bennett   Take it out of the wallet

Chadwick   No.

Bennett   Now. Hole-head.

Thank you.

And give it to William. He's a bit short.

Chadwick *gives the money to* **William.**

Bennett *watches. Has another drink.*

Silence.

Some time.

They all try not to move, apart from **Bennett***, who moves with some comfort.*

Bennett   It's warmer today. I think. Don't you, Chadwick? Haven't you noticed it's warmer today? They would put the heating on just as the sun comes out. How typical is that?

An Indian summer.

We're going to the dentist this afternoon. I've got the afternoon off. I'm looking forward to that. Hang out in the sunshine.

My mum's already here to collect me. I saw her. She's waiting in the reception. I decided to just walk straight past her.

Everybody's being very quiet.

How's the revision going, Lilly? Have you started yet?

Lilly   Yes.

Bennett   Sorry? You're muttering. I didn't hear you.

Lilly   I said yes. Of course I've started. The exams are next week.

Bennett *nods his head.*

He goes to **Chadwick***.*

He stares at him. He touches his cheek.

Bennett   Lovely.

What did you have this morning, Chadders?

What subject did you have?

Chadwick   Maths.

Bennett   Maths. Very good. Very good.

I had Politics.

He burps in **Chadwick***'s face.*

Lucy Francis *enters. She's eleven. She is nervous in the room. The others notice her.*

Lucy   Mum says you've got to hurry up.

Bennett *turns to her.*

Bennett   Right. Thank you, Lucy. Tell her I'm coming.

He collects his bag and jacket. He gives **William** *his drink back. He stops right in front of* **Tanya***.*

Bennett   What's the matter with you?

Tanya   Nothing.

Bennett   You look all sad. Are you really sad?

Tanya   No.

Bennett   You are though, aren't you? Do you know why? Do you want to know why you're so sad? Should I tell you?

You're sad because you're fat.

You're fat because you eat too much.

You eat too much because you're depressed. You're depressed because of the fucking world.

Right. My dentist awaits these elegant gnashers.

He gnashes his teeth at **Chadwick**. *Leaves.*

Tanya   Are you OK?

Chadwick   What?

Tanya   Are you OK, I asked.

Chadwick   Of course. Yes. I'm fine. Of course I'm OK.

Tanya   I'm really sorry. I tried to stop him.

Chadwick   Yes. I know. You don't need to –

The bell goes.

They all wait for a beat. **Lilly**'*s looking at* **Cissy**.

Cissy   What?

He was messing about.

Fucking hell. It was a joke.

He's just nervous. He's terrified of the dentist.

Are you coming to English?

Tanya *looks at her. Says nothing.*

Cissy   I'll walk with you.

Tanya *nods. Exits.* **Cissy** *follows.*

Lilly   What are you going to do?

About your money?

William   Did you take it?

Lilly   What?

William   I just wondered if you'd taken it. You might have done. You never know. You might have gone into my bag and found it.

Lilly   What are you talking about?

William   Ha!

Lilly   What?

William   Tricked you!

Lilly   You what?

William   I'm just winding you up, Lilly. Just having a little joke. Do *you* want some of this?

He drinks some more Campari and offers her the bottle.

Lilly   No, thank you. I'll see you later.

William   Yeah. I look forward to that.

She leaves. Some time.

Chadwick   How was your mock?

William   It was good. It was Lloyd. He was very sharp. He's by some distance my favourite teacher. He gave me a cigarette at the end which was probably a bit unprofessional of him. But quite sweet as well.

When's yours?

Chadwick   I'm not doing a mock. I'm just going to go down and do the interview.

William   Right.

He reaches into his own wallet and gives **Chadwick** *the twenty pounds.*

Chadwick   Thank you.

William   That's all right.

Chadwick   He's –

William   Yeah.

Chadwick   I don't think I deserve some of the things that happen to me, you know?

Do you?

I don't think I'm so bad. I'm not as bad they make out. I'm not as stupid as people think.

William   I don't think anybody thinks for a second that you're stupid in any way.

Chadwick *gets his phone out. He opens it. He finds a text. He reads it and shows it to* **William.**

William   When did you get this?

Chadwick   This one came this morning.

William   This isn't from Bennett, is it?

Chadwick   No. It's probably from somebody downstairs. That's why I come up here all the time.

William   Have you had this kind of thing before?

You should tell somebody about it. This is serious, Chadwick.

Chadwick   Yeah.

Sometimes . . .

William   What?

Chadwick   Nothing.

William   Go on. Chadwick, what were you going to say?

Chadwick   There's far, far less antimatter in the universe than there is matter. Did you know that?

William   I'm not entirely sure that I did, Chadwick, no. Was that really what you were going to say?

Chadwick   Yes. That's one of the things that the experiments at CERN are investigating.

William   CERN?

Chadwick   The LHC?

The Large Hadron Collider?

William   That broken telescope?

Chadwick   It's not a telescope. It's an atomic particle accelerator.

William   That they couldn't even get working.

Chadwick   But they will.

His conviction stops **William** *for a beat.*

Chadwick   One of the things that this collider may be able to test is where all the antimatter has gone to. Some people think that it must be somewhere. That it can't just disappear. Given its absence from the known universe they speculate that this proves that there are alternative universes. And that the antimatter resides in these alternative universes.

I think the experiments that this telescope is able to develop will prove them right. Eventually.

It makes me feel rather small. We're so little. We take up a tiny amount of space, as individuals, don't we? And a negligible amount of time.

If it was possible to harness antimatter and to bring a single antimatter positron into contact with a single electron of matter it would create an explosion of untold force and energy. They could build an antimatter bomb. It would be forty thousand times bigger than a nuclear bomb.

I think that'd be better.

Don't you think it'd be better sometimes? Just to end it.

I do. I think about that far more than I ought to. I sometimes think that when you die it's like you cross this threshold. You cross this door. You get out of here.

Some time.

William   There are other ways. Of getting out, you know.

Chadwick nods.

When I'm twenty one I'm going to inherit over half a million pounds. Did you know that? Did I ever tell you that?

Chadwick   No.

William   My dad made over twelve million pounds in the oil markets in Russia in the early nineties. He left half a million pounds of it to me in trust in his will. I inherit it when I'm twenty-one. I can do whatever I want with it.

I'm moving to New York. I'm going to go and live with Lilly.

Chadwick *looks at him.*

William   We've planned it. Ask her if you don't believe me. We're going to get a warehouse loft conversion in the Lower East Side of Manhattan. I'm going to get a Lamborghini Esprit. Lilly'll probably get a haircut like Jennifer Aniston or something like that. We'll drive around. That'll be better than being dead, I think.

Chadwick   Won't Nicholas mind?

William   What?

Chadwick   Won't Nicholas mind you living with Lilly?

William   What has it got to do with him?

Chadwick   She's going out with him.

William   Who is?

Chadwick   Lilly. She's been fucking him is what I heard.

William   She's not.

Chadwick   She has.

William   Since when?

Chadwick   Since about the first week she got here.

Pause.

William   Oh.

Chadwick   Didn't you know?

William   No. I didn't.

Chadwick   Has it come as something of a blow?

William   Well. I admit I am a little disappointed.

Silence. Some time.

Can I stay at yours tonight?

Chadwick   What?

William   Can I stay at your house tonight?

Chadwick   I don't know.

William   What would your parents say if I just came round?

Chadwick   I'm not sure they'd like it. With the exams next week and everything.

William   They wouldn't do anything though, would they?

Chadwick   I don't know.

William   I could sleep on your floor. We could top and tail. We could get up in the middle of the night and make cheese on toast and eat it.

Chadwick   No.

William   What are you like at home?

Chadwick   I don't know.

William   Are you different?

Chadwick   I don't think so.

William   Do you behave differently than you do here? I bet you do. Do people like you there a bit more? I bet they do, don't they?

Why won't you let me stay then?

Chadwick   It's not about letting you do anything. It's just not really my house.

William   I could come round after the exams then. Couldn't I?

You know what it is that's wrong with your bone structure? I just figured it out. It's your nose. It's a little bit too high up your face, I think. Isn't it? A bit too high up there?

I'm going to be fucking really fucking late now. I've got lessons all afternoon.

I have to say I feel like you've really let me down.

Scene Four

'The Woman Inside' by Cows.

It's Monday 10 November, 8.27 a.m.

Bennett, Tanya, Nicholas, Cissy, William *and* **Lilly** *are in the common room.*

Bennett   What?

Tanya   A wasp!

Cissy   Where?

Tanya   There.

Cissy   Fuck.

Nicholas   That's not a wasp.

Cissy   Of course it's a wasp. Fuck.

Tanya   Get rid of it.

Nicholas   It's the middle of November. It's a fly.

Tanya   It's a wasp, you fucking idiot. Open a window.

William   I can't see it.

Nicholas   'Fucking idiot', that's a bit strong.

Cissy   There. My God, it's by your head.

Tanya   It's gonna sting me.

Cissy   Get it. Kill it. Fuck!

William   Don't kill it.

Cissy   What?

William   Don't kill it.

Tanya   Has it gone yet?

William   You mustn't kill it. It's a living creature.

Cissy   Are you being serious?

Bennett   It's a fucking wasp.

Nicholas   Just open the window.

Bennett   Wait.

Tanya   William, please will you open the window?

Bennett   Hold on. Watch.

Cissy   Bennett.

Bennett   Trust me. Watch.

Tanya   William, open the window.

Bennett   No. Don't. William. Don't. Watch this.

He moves to grab the wasp in his hand.

He moves suddenly and with some elegance.

He squeezes his fist closed.

Opens it.

He has caught and killed the dead wasp.

The others look at him and at the wasp. He plucks it from his fist and holds it between two fingers.

Cissy   Oh my God.

Nicholas   How did you do that?

Bennett   Magic. My dad taught me. You just have to watch the way they move.

Tanya   That's freaky.

He looks at her.

Bennett   You want to hold it?

Tanya   No, thank you. It's really odd.

William   I don't think it's odd. I think it's cruel.

Bennett *looks at the dead wasp. He gives it to* **William***.* **William** *takes it. Looks at it.*

Puts it in his pocket.

Cissy   Cruel? How's it cruel? Wasps are vicious, pointless things.

Nicholas   It's pretty fucking impressive is what it is.

Cissy   Didn't it sting you?

Chadwick *enters.*

Bennett   Chadwick.

Stand there.

Now wait there.

Thanks.

No. They never do. Not if you're quick enough.

Chadwick   Lloyd's had a heart attack.

Everybody turns to look at him.

Eliot just told me. He's in Stepping Hill. He nearly died. He didn't. They don't know how long he'll be in there.

Bennett   Wow.

William   What did you say?

Chadwick   Late last night. Lloyd. He had a heart attack.

William   A heart attack?

Chadwick   It was quite severe. I think there were complications. Eliot said that somebody told him that he'd lost complete consciousness for a few seconds.

Tanya   Jesus.

William   Lloyd?

Chadwick   That's what I said.

William   Is he dead?

Chadwick   No. He's in hospital.

William   But he died? For a bit?

Chadwick   No. He lost consciousness, that's different from dying.

Bennett   You can't die for a bit.

William   I saw him yesterday.

Chadwick   Yes.

William   I don't believe you.

Chadwick   I'm not lying, honestly.

Pause.

Cissy   Fucking hell, eh?

Tanya   At his age. With that level of smoking. That's serious. And it's the History exam this afternoon as well.

Pause.

Bennett   Do you know what I liked about him?

William   He's not dead.

Bennett   I always liked the way he moved his hands. He had these little jerky movements. They were charming. Oooh! They'd take you by surprise.

William   Don't talk about him like he's dead. He's not dead.

Cissy   I'm not surprised teachers have heart attacks. They wander round like trauma victims. You look into their eyes. They're terrified. They all end up with stomach ulcers. They all suffer uncontrollable sweating. They haven't got a clue who half of the school is. It's ridiculous. They're the ones who are meant to be looking after us.

William   I'm going to go and see him. Does anybody want to come with me?

Does anybody want to come with me to see him?

Tanya   It's half eight, William.

William   What?

Tanya   Maybe after school. We could go. We don't know what time visiting is.

William   What?

Tanya   I'm not entirely sure he'll be able to take visitors for a couple of days. My grandad was like that. They kept him sleeping, mainly.

Bennett   Did I tell you you could fucking move.

Did I?

Chadwick   No.

Bennett   Then what the fuck are you moving for?

Chadwick   I wanted to put my stuff in my locker.

Bennett   Well you can't. Today, Chadwick, as a little tribute to a dying Lloyd, you are my doll. Do you understand me?

Tanya   Bennett.

Bennett   What? What, Tanya?

Tanya   Leave him alone. It's boring.

Bennett   Boring? I'm not bored. Are you bored, Chadwick? Are you bored, Nicky?

Tanya   You're such a –

Bennett   What?

What am I such a, Tanya? Come and tell me.

Ah. Fuck it. I'm playing. I'm playing. I'm being a prick.

Chadwick. Come in. Come in, lovely boy. Put your stuff away I'm being an arsehole.

How are you today, Chadders?

Chadwick   I'm fine, thank you.

Bennett   Ready for your General Studies exam?

Chadwick   Yes.

Bennett   Me too, lovely, me too. It's my last one. I'm tempted to do it with my eyes closed.

That's awful fucking horrible news about Lloyd, isn't it? I wonder what he looked like. I wonder if he stopped breathing. I wonder what colour he went. Have you ever seen anybody die, Chadders?

Chadwick   No.

Bennett   I heard you get an erection. Is he too old to get an erection, do you think?

Cissy   Bennett.

Bennett   I bet he's got a fucking huge cock. A really fucking big schlong, don't you think, Chadders?

Tanya   You're sick.

Bennett   Have you ever had an erection, Chadwick?

Tanya   Don't.

Bennett   What? I'm only asking. I'm only asking my mate Chadders.

Have you, Chadwick? Have you ever had an erection, Chadwick?

Have you ever come?

Chadwick   Yes.

Bennett   How do you know?

Chadwick   It's obvious, isn't it? Don't you know that?

Bennett   I can't imagine you coming. Do you wank all the time at home, Chadwick? What do you think about when you're having a wank? Do you think about girls or boys?

Chadwick   I think about girls. Don't you?

Bennett   Your mum doesn't count, Chadwick, can I just say that?

Or do you think about fat little Tanya mainly? You're in there, mate, by the way. You should definitely ask her out. You'd make a lovely couple.

Have you ever had a girlfriend, Chadwick? Chadwick, answer my fucking question, you uptight prick cunt.

Chadwick   What?

Bennett   Chadwick, have you ever had a girlfriend in your whole fucking life?

Chadwick   No. I haven't. Not yet.

Cissy   Ah!

Bennett   They will drop off eventually, you know? They'll dry up and drop off. Like dead fruit.

Cissy   That's not true. Don't listen to him.

Bennett   What do you think, Nicky? Poor lamb's never been kissed.

Nicholas *doesn't answer.*

Cissy   God. Can you imagine? Doing it with Chadwick. Sorry, Chadwick. No offence or anything.

Chadwick   No. None taken.

Bennett   You should give him some tips, Nicky. You get fucked all the time is what I heard.

Nicholas   Who told you that?

Bennett   Everybody knows about that, don't they, Lilly?

(*To* **Tanya**.) I can't believe you're being such a cock tease with him. It's fucking cruel if you ask me. (*To* **Nicholas**.) Haven't you got any mates who are interested in charity work?

Nicholas   No, Bennett. I haven't.

Bennett   Couldn't you ask Copley for him?

Cissy   Have you seen her face?

Bennett   Have you seen her cunt?

Her cunt is so fat.

Tanya   This is just –

Bennett   Do you know what that means, Chadwick? A fat cunt like that?

You don't, do you?

Mind you, you wouldn't know what to do with it, Chadwick, would you, son? If she came up to you and bent over your desk in the middle of Physics to mark your work you wouldn't have a clue where to start.

Chadwick   And you would?

Bennett   What did you say?

Chadwick   I said, 'And you would?' Know where to start. Bennett.

Bennett   I don't believe you said that out loud.

Chadwick   If she leant over your desk in the middle of Physics what are you saying you'd do?

Bennett   I'd fuck her until she fucking screamed.

Chadwick   Does that mean you're bisexual?

A pause.

Bennett   Tanya, have you got some lipstick.

Tanya   What?

Bennett   Have you? Have you got any lipstick, Tanya?

Cissy   Bennett, the bell's about to go. Everybody'll come out.

Bennett   Can I ask you something, Tanya old girl? Do you think I feel bad about myself because you keep on sticking up for him? Is that what you think?

He goes to **Chadwick***. He grabs a fistful of his hair, really tightly.*

Bennett   Tanya. Take your lipstick out or I'll properly hurt him.

There.

Now Chadwick, come over to Tanya. And she'll put some lipstick on for you.

Tanya   What?

Bennett   Come on Tanya.

Cissy   Oh my God.

Bennett   Chadwick, come to Tanya. Purse your lips.

Tanya.

He spits in her face.

Do it.

Now.

Thank you.

Chadwick   It's nice.

Cissy   What?

Chadwick   I like it. It smells nice.

Bennett   You look so fucking gay, Chadwick, you make me want to do a piss.

Kiss him.

Cissy   What?

Bennett   Kiss him. For me.

She looks at **Bennett***. She goes to* **Chadwick***. She kisses him with a real sexuality.*

Bennett   What are you doing William?

William   Just having a bit of a dance.

Bennett *watches* **Cissy** *kiss* **Chadwick***.*

Bennett   Hey, Chadwick. That's my girlfriend.

Chadwick *and* **Cissy** *stop kissing*

Bennett   What the fuck are you doing, kissing my fucking girlfriend?

Chadwick   You told me to.

Cissy   He tasted like crisps.

Bennett   Right in front of me.

Chadwick   You told me to, Bennett. I didn't want to.

Bennett   You didn't want to? What are you saying? What are you saying about Cissy, Chadwick? Are you calling her? First you snog her right in front of me and then you go and call her like that. I should cut your face off for that. I should cut your ears off. I should cut your needle dick off. You fucking pervert fuckhead cunt.

William   Stop it, Bennett.

Bennett   What?

William   Stop it.

Just leave him alone.

Bennett   Are you actually talking to *me* now?

William   You're a complete fucking prick. Leave him alone.

Bennett   Listen to him.

William   I mean it, Bennett. Leave him alone. Now.

Bennett   Listen to the brother fucker over here.

William   What did you say?

Bennett   Oh, I think you heard me, William, didn't you?

William   Come here. Come here and say that.

Bennett   I said, 'Listen to the brother fucker over here.' I was talking about you. I was referring to your brother.

William   I'll kill you for that.

Lilly   William, calm down. He was winding you up.

William   Yeah, well, I'll wind him up. I'll wind him up like a knot.

The bell goes.

They go to move.

Where are you all fucking going? Stay there. Stay there, Bennett. I'm not scared of you. I'm not scared of anybody. You want to know how hard I am?

Lilly   William. It's registration.

William   Come on, Bennet. You cunt. You fuckhead. Come on then. Any time. You and me. Outside. Now.

Bennett   Have you heard him?

Cissy   He's talking like a comic book.

Bennett   You're talking like a character from a film.

William   I could beat you in a fight really easily.

Bennett   I'm sure you could.

William   I tell you. One day, soon, you are going to get the surprise of your life. (*To* **Chadwick**.) Don't listen to him. He's worth nothing. He's just a big empty vacuous awful space.

Chadwick   I don't mind.

Bennett   Don't you?

Chadwick   I don't worry about you lot any more.

Bennett   Well. That's big of you.

Chadwick   Human beings are pathetic. Everything human beings do finishes up bad in the end. Everything good human beings ever make is built on something monstrous. Nothing lasts. We certainly won't. We could have made something really extraordinary and we won't. We've been around one hundred thousand years. We'll have died out before the next two hundred. You know what we've got to look forward to? You know what will define the next two hundred years? Religions will become brutalised; crime rates will become hysterical; everybody will become addicted to internet sex; suicide will become fashionable; there'll be famine; there'll be floods; there'll be fires in the major cities of the Western world. Our education systems will become battered. Our health services unsustainable; our police forces unmanageable; our governments corrupt. There'll be open brutality in the streets; there'll be nuclear war; massive depletion of resources on every level; insanely increasing third-world population. It's happening already. It's happening now. Thousands die every summer from floods in the Indian monsoon season. Africans from Senegal wash up on the beaches of the Mediterranean and get looked after by guilty liberal holidaymakers. Somalians wait in hostels in Malta or prison islands north of Australia. Hundreds die of heat or fire every year in Paris. Or California. Or Athens. The oceans will rise. The cities will flood. The power stations will flood. Airports will flood. Species will vanish for ever. Including ours. So if you think I'm worried by you calling me names, Bennet, you little, little boy, you are fucking kidding yourself.

Bennett Blimey.

That's a bit bleak, Chadwick.

Chadwick Just because something's bleak doesn't mean it's not true.

Cissy I don't believe that.

Chadwick You should do.

Cissy We can educate each other.

Chadwick We don't.

Cissy We can change things.

Chadwick We can't.

Cissy We can. There's science. There's technology.

Chadwick   It won't help now.

Cissy   People have always said the world's going to end.

Chadwick   They were wrong. I'm really fucking not.

I was right about your lipstick, too, Tanya. It does taste nice.

He licks his own lips. Leaves.

Bennett   Ah! First period! Once more into the breach. What time's the exam?

Ten o'clock, isn't it? Lovely. That was fun that, William. I rather enjoyed myself. Same time tomorrow, old bean?

Until the exam hall, lovelies. Don't be late.

He leaves.

Cissy   We've got English.

No response.

We'll be late.

No response.

At least he'll notice you.

Tanya *leaves.*

Cissy *stands for a while. She has no idea where to go or what to say or what to do.*

She leaves.

Nicholas   Are you all right?

William   Am I what?

Nicholas   I was asking if you were OK.

William   Do I not look it?

Lilly   It's good that you stood up to him.

William   Are you both free now?

Lilly   Until the exam.

William   Well. You'll like that.

Nicholas   I can't believe they make us do a lesson. For one period . . .

William   Have they turned the heating off in here?

Nicholas   No. I'm really warm.

Lilly   I'm boiling.

William *looks at her.*

William   I feel a little bit let down.

Lilly   What by? What by, William?

William   It's hard because there are some things that have happened that are entirely my fault.

Lilly   What like?

William   You know what like.

Lilly   I don't.

William   All of you talk about it all the time.

I'm not that naive. I know I might look it. I know I might look like 'oh William'. William Billiam. William Tell. William the thick. William the Great. Do you think I'm William Shakespeare?

They look at him.

Because I might be. It's entirely possible. Look at the news!

Nicholas   What?

William   A hundred and ninety people were killed yesterday in a plane crash in Brazil. Why do you think that happened?

Lilly   It skidded. On the runway. The runway was wet.

William   Oh right. Yeah.

Nicholas   That's true.

William   That's what they tell you is true.

Nicholas   Are you saying you caused the plane crash, William?

William   Wouldn't you like to know?

I bet you really –

How long have you been going out, you two?

Nicholas   William.

William   Why the fuck won't anybody come with me to Lloyd's funeral, for fucksake!

Lilly   He's not dead. He didn't die. Chadwick said –

William   They should close the whole school is what they fucking well should do.

How many times have you fucked her, Nicholas?

Nicholas   William, shut up.

William   Or what? Is his cock really huge?

Lilly   Be quiet. You're making a fool of yourself.

William   What?

What?

Have I said something really embarrassing?

I'm sorry.

God.

I'm really sorry. I didn't even hear myself speak.

Come here. Come here, Lilly. My best friend.

Lilly   William, get off.

He kisses the side of her head.

William   I could eat you. I'd better go now.

Lilly   William, where are you going?

William   I'm going to go and see Lloyd. Get a bit of conversation. Bit of stimulation. You know what I mean?

Lilly You've got your exams.

William I've got what?

Lilly You've got the General Studies exam. You've got History this afternoon.

William *looks at her briefly, slightly confused by what she's talking about. Then he leaves.*

They watch him go.

They look at each other.

Nicholas Are you OK?

Lilly I think so. Are you?

He nods. They hold each other's gaze for a while.

Scene Five

'Fell in Love With a Girl' by The White Stripes.

It's Monday 10 November, 4.38 p.m.

Lilly What?

What?

Aren't you going to talk to me?

Are you just going to look at me, William, because it's creeping me out a bit?

Why are all the windows open? Did you open them?

What did you want? Where have you been all day?

Look. I got your text. You asked me to come here so I came.

It's getting dark. I'm going to go home unless you speak to me. I mean it.

William Lloyd died. This morning. When we were in here.

I went up to the hospital after I left you and Nicholas. I was too late. I tried to get you all to come earlier. You all stopped me.

It was a horrible place.

He's the second person I ever met who's died now. How many people do you know who've died?

I was meant to have exams, wasn't I? I got lost coming home. I was wandering around.

Have I missed them? My exams? Did I miss History?

Lilly *nods.*

William   While I was wandering about I realised something about you. I realised what you are. In real life. It came to me. Like an epiphany.

Lilly   What are you talking about?

William   You're a robot, aren't you?

Lilly   What?

William   Where did they make you? What laboratory did they make you in?

When I asked you out, were you already going out with Nicholas?

You were, weren't you? Why didn't you tell me? Why didn't you say anything about it?

Can you hear that?

Lilly   What?

William   That banging?

Lilly   No.

William   Are you lying?

Lilly   I didn't know what to say. I really liked you. I really like you. I didn't want to let you down.

William   Good answer. I brought you a present when I was out and about. It's a very early Christmas present.

Lilly   Fucking hell.

William 'Fucking hell.' If my mum could hear you swearing.

Lilly You can't give me this.

William 'You can't give me this.' Yes I can. I just did. I got one too. I got some CDs. Look I burnt them on for you.

Lilly William, there's three hundred songs on here.

William 'William there's a hundred songs on there.' Ha!

Lilly Did you buy all these?

William 'Did you buy all these?'

Lilly I thought you said your mum was dead.

William My stepmum.

Don't.

Lilly What?

William Look at me like that. You look exactly like her. I really hate it

Will you do me a favour? In return for my present?

Lilly It depends what it is.

William Will you stop burning yourself? Because I don't think it's very good for you. I think you'd be better off stopping.

Will you, Lilly? Do you promise?

A long pause.

Lilly I'll try.

William Try really hard.

Lilly William, are you alright?

William I'm just a bit.

Lilly What?

William I can't think of the word.

Lilly   For what?

William   When you haven't slept enough?

Lilly   Tired?

William   Yes. I'm a bit tired.

Lilly   You couldn't remember the word 'tired.'

William   Do you know what I figured out?

Lilly   What?

William   That it's not me. It's not my fault. It's not a problem of genetics, it's a problem of geography. It's Manchester. It's Stockport.

Lilly   What is?

William   You go downtown. Yes? You go down to the Arndale. Yes? All the kids in there look like they could slice your stomach open and reach their hands inside your stomach and pull your insides out. Yes?

Lilly   They don't.

William   You walk into a room. Yes? Everybody knows you've walked into that room. Everybody's waiting for you. All these people are waiting for you. Aren't they? With their legs and their arms and their hair hanging down in front of their faces when they cry.

Some of the things you told me weren't true.

Lilly   What things?

William   You know what things. There's a lot about you which is a lie. The way you tie your tie is a lie. You're lying with the way you tie your fucking tie.

Lilly   This is exhausting me.

William   Yeah.

Lilly   I'm going home.

William   Don't.

Lilly   Why shouldn't I?

William   I'm scared of what I might do if you leave.

She looks at him.

Lilly   Yeah.

We all get scared William.

Sometimes the world is a bit unnerving. Some people do awful things but, and you need to listen to this William, seriously, most of the time the world is all right. You need to get that into your head and stop moping about.

William   Moping? Is that what you think I'm doing?

Lilly   Most people are all right.

William   They're not.

Lilly   They're funny. They chat a bit. They tell jokes. They're kind. They're all right.

William   You so should have gone to the College, shouldn't you?

Lilly   You know, ninety nine per cent of the people in the school are perfectly good people. Ninety nine per cent of the young people in this country, William, and nobody ever says this, ninety nine percent of the young people in this country do a really good job at the actual work of being alive. They'll survive. Happily. They'll grow up. They'll end up doing jobs. Being married. Living lives which are perfectly good and reasonable and all right and happy ones. That's not a bad thing William. You know? What makes you think you're any different? What makes you think you're so special? When I was ten −

William   When you were what?

Lilly   Listen to me. I'm trying to tell you something. When I was ten I used to get headaches.

William   What are you talking about?

Lilly   They were properly fierce. It used to feel as though the front of my head was being carved in two. They could really bring tears to my eyes. I didn't tell my mum about them for weeks –

William   Why are you telling me this?

Lilly   But after about two weeks I did.

William   I think you've gone a bit mad.

Lilly   I told her. She took me to the doctor and the doctor gave me some aspirin and told me to drink more water and get some more fresh air and to eat less sugar and so I did and the headaches went away.

William   I'm not talking about headaches. This is more than a headache.

Lilly   Maybe you should tell somebody.

William   Are you trying to inspire me? With your little tiny story? You want to inspire me? Take your top off. That'll inspire me. Let me see your tits. That'd be a massive inspiration I think. That'd really cheer me up, Lilly. Honestly.

Lilly   I'm sorry I didn't want to go out with you. I wanted to go out with Nicholas instead.

I really love him.

But I always thought you'd be my mate. And I would still really like to be in spite of everything. Because actually I think you're not that well and I'm worried about you and I want to get you some help.

William   Ha!

Lilly   What?

William   Can I ask you this: when you have sex with him, with Nicholas, does it hurt?

Does it?

Please tell me.

Lilly   No.

William   Doesn't it?

Lilly   No.

William   What's it like?

Lilly   It's lovely.

William   Right. That's good. That's good for you. I don't
like him. Personally. I think he's a fraud. I think he's a liar.
I think he's made of lies and shit. But that's just my opinion.

Lilly   He isn't.

William   I am completely entitled to my own opinion.
Don't you dare try to tell me that I'm not because I fucking am.

Some time.

Lilly   Nicholas told me that you were lying about your
parents.

Why did you lie about your parents, William?

William   I didn't. I wasn't. I didn't lie.

Lilly   He told me your parents are still alive but that you
had a brother and it was your brother who died when he was
a baby.

William   Lies, damn lies and statistics.

Lilly   Why did you lie about it, William?

Why did you lie about your parents being dead?

Is it true about your brother?

Did you have a brother who died? Why did your brother die?

William   Can you hear it?

Lilly   What?

William   I can hear it again. That banging.

Lilly   I can't hear it at all.

William   There was a boy killed himself here once. When it was a boys' school. He climbed onto the roof of the quad. Jumped off. This was back in the seventies. Maybe it's him.

Were there a lot of gypsies in Cambridge?

Lilly   What?

William   We should sort them out, us two, I reckon. Go on a march.

Lilly   Sort who out?

William   I know we could. When two people love each other as much as we do then I think they can do anything.

Lilly   I don't love you.

William   You must do.

Lilly   I don't, William

A long pause. Longer than you think you can get away with.

William *turns the lights off. He stands still for a long time.*

Lilly   Can you turn the light back on please, William?

William   I'm sorry. Did you say something?

Lilly   You're starting to −

William   I don't blame you. By the way. I'm rubbish, me. I'm a waste of time. I'm not even worth the space I take up. I'm not even worth the paper I'm written on. I've got no friends. I've got no imagination. I've got no ideas.

Lilly   Stop it.

William   I hate my shoes. I hate my house. I hate this school. I hate my hair. Can I have a haircut?

Lilly   What?

William   Will you give me a haircut, please? A better one. One that makes me look less of a fucking spastic −

Lilly   Don't say that.

William   – than this haircut makes me look.

Lilly   I hate that word.

William   Cut my hair.

Lilly   With what?

William   I don't care. Your hands. Your ruler. Pull it out.

I'm just. I want it to stop.

You know when I'm with you?

Lilly   I've only known you a month.

William   I feel like I'm earthed. Here.

He touches the side of her head with the palm of his hand. Nothing apparently happens or changes.

And watch what happens if I let go.

He lets go.

See?

Nothing apparently happens or changes. He smiles for a while. He stops smiling quite suddenly.

Who are you?

Lilly   What?

William   I don't know who you are.

Lilly   –

William   Can I tell you something?

Lilly   What?

William   Do you want a word of advice? A word to the wise?

Lilly   –

William   Tomorrow.

Lilly   What?

William   Don't come into school.

Scene Six

'Touch Me I'm Sick' by Mudhoney.

It's Tuesday 11 November, 8.57 a.m.

The stage remains empty for a while. **Bennett** *enters. Then* **Nicholas**.

Bennett   They've marked the exams.

Nicholas *looks at him for a while.*

Nicholas   What?

Bennett   I just saw Gilchrist. She said she'll give us our results later.

Nicholas   Fuck.

Bennett   Yeah. She had a remarkable look on her face. It was like a combination of glee and fury.

I absolutely know that I have really properly fucked them all up.

My parents will go fucking mental.

Nicholas   Yeah.

Bennett   They'll drag out the same old speeches. About the fees. Do you know what we have to do to get the money to send you to that place? Do you have the slightest idea how much it costs every year?

I don't actually. Do you?

Nicholas   Have you seen Lilly?

Bennett   I've not seen anybody all morning. Maybe they're all hiding. Maybe they all know something we don't.

Aren't you worried at all about your results?

Nicholas   Too late to change anything now.

Bennett   Well that's very fucking mature I have to say.

He lights a cigarette.

He looks at **Nicholas**.

Bennett   How are things going with her? With Lilly?

Nicholas   They're all right, thank you.

Bennett   She's lovely.

Nicholas   Yes. She is.

Bennett   She's surprisingly smart. I like her cos she's rock hard. She's very lucky.

Did you hear that Tanya's dad came up to the school?

Nicholas   Lilly mentioned that she'd seen him.

Bennett   Yesterday lunchtime he came and spoke to Edwards. She must have rung him during the day. The fat bitch. He kept me here till half past six last night. Bastard. He was probably marking our exams while I was sat there doing fucking lines.

Nicholas   You shouldn't have spat at her.

Bennett *looks at* **Nicholas** *for a beat.*

Bennett   No. I shouldn't have done.

It was stupid. I just really wanted to. I wanted to try it out. I wanted to know what it would feel like.

Do you ever get things like that?

Nicholas   I'm not sure.

Bennett   Have you ever wanted to set fire to things?

Nicholas   Nothing serious. Maybe the occasional dustbin.

Bennett   Have you ever wanted to blow something up?

Nicholas   Fuck, yeah. Who hasn't?

Bennett   Have you ever wanted to kiss a boy?

Nicholas   No.

Bennett   Never?

Nicholas   No.

Bennett   Liar.

Nicholas   I'm not lying.

Bennett   I wanted to kiss Thom Yorke once.

Nicholas   Yeah?

Bennett   And David Bowie.

Nicholas *looks at him for a beat. Smiles at him.*

Pause.

Nicholas   I was so hungover this morning I couldn't believe it.

Bennett   Where were you last night?

Nicholas   I went out with my brother. He's come home for Christmas.

Bennett   Already? Fucking students. How is he?

Nicholas   He's really well. Mum and Dad are happy to see him.

Bennett   How's Durham?

Nicholas   He loves it, I think.

Bennett   That's good. Are you all going away for Christmas or something?

Nicholas   I don't think so.

Bennett   We're going to fucking Reykjavik of all places.

Nicholas *looks at him. Smiles.*

Nicholas   I shouldn't have been drinking. I'm on painkillers for my ankle. I feel fucking shit now.

Bennett   What happened to your ankle?

Nicholas   I twisted it. Playing rugby.

Bennett   When was this?

Nicholas   Last week.

Bennett   You never told me this.

Nicholas *looks at him.*

Bennett   Can I see it?

Nicholas *shows him his ankle.*

Bennett   It looks red, Nicholas.

Nicholas   Yeah. You should have seen it last week.

Bennett *touches it. He winces as he touches it as though feeling* **Nicholas***'s pain.*

Nicholas   It's all right. It doesn't really hurt any more.

Cissy *enters.*

Cissy   Don't tell my mum. Don't tell my mum. Don't tell my mum. Don't tell my mum.

Nicholas   Don't tell your mum what?

Cissy   I just saw Anderson. I got a 'B' for English.

Bennett   Fucking hell.

Cissy   I know.

Nicholas   A 'B' 's not bad.

Cissy   Are you being serious?

Nicholas   A 'B' 's good I think.

Cissy   If she finds out she'll kill me.

Nicholas   Cissy, I think you're exaggerating.

Bennett   You don't know her mother.

Cissy   How can I stop her from finding out?

Nicholas   Don't tell her.

Cissy   She'll get the report.

Bennett   Hide it. Burn it.

Cissy   Don't be fucking stupid, Bennett. She knows there'll be a report. It's the end of the term. There's always a report.

Bennett Tipp-Ex over it.

Cissy Oh you're *so* not helping.

Tanya *enters.*

Tanya What is the matter with you?

Cissy I got my English results.

Tanya Already?

Bennett She got a 'B'.

Tanya Ouch! Have you ever got a 'B' in anything before?

Nicholas She's worried her mother's going to kill her.

Tanya Yeah. She will.

Cissy If I fuck up –

Bennett You already have, sweetheart.

Cissy No, properly. If I properly fuck up. If I don't get the grades I need for my place in the summer, not in the mocks, in the real exams, then I'll go –

I don't know what I'll do.

Tanya You won't. Fuck up. You're being really stupid. These are just mocks.

Cissy I'll never get out of Stockport. I'll never leave. I'll be stuck here for ever. There's a whole world out there and I'll never see it once, not ever. All these things I want to do, I won't be able to do them.

Tanya You keep going on about that.

Cissy *looks at her.*

Tanya It's not about Stockport, Cissy. It's about you. You were made here. You keep trying to pretend that you weren't. It's ridiculous.

The two girls look at each other.

Cissy I don't know what to say.

And I don't know what you're laughing at.

Bennett What?

Cissy You're meant to be my boyfriend.

Bennett Oh, come on!

Cissy You're meant to stick up for me.

Bennett It was funny. She was being funny.

Cissy All you ever do is laugh at me.

Bennett Well. Can you blame me?

Cissy What?

Bennett You *are* ridiculous. For somebody so clever you're unbelievably fucking stupid. How could I fail to laugh at you?

Isn't she? Isn't she Nicky?

Chadwick *enters.*

Bennett Chadwick, isn't Cissy fucking ridiculous?

Chadwick I don't think so. She's always seemed rather intelligent to me.

Bennett I'm not denying that. I'm not talking about her intelligence for fuck sake.

William *enters.*

Bennett William. Answer me this. Why is it that every single person in this school judges everybody else by the level of their intelligence? Not by their wit. Not by their appearance. Not by their dress sense. Not by their taste in music. By how many 'A*'s they got at GCSE.

William *pulls a gun out of the inside pocket of his blazer.*

William I've no idea.

He shoots his gun at the lights in the common room. He smashes the bulbs.

The room darkens.

It works then.

I did warn you, Bennett. Don't say I didn't warn you because I really fucking did.

He points his gun at **Bennett**.

Bennett   What? What the fuck? No. No. God. Please. Don't.

Bennett *cowers away from him. Wherever he goes to,* **William** *follows him with his gun.*

Nicholas   William.

William *turns to look at him. Points the gun at him when he does.*

William   Yeah. What?

Nicholas   Don't.

William   Don't what?

Tanya *has started crying.* **Cissy** *moves to the door.*

William   Don't. Cissy. Fucking just don't.

Nicholas   William. People will come.

William   What?

Nicholas   People will have heard the gunshot. They'll be here any second.

William   Do you think so?

I can't hear anybody coming. Can you hear anybody?

They listen.

Nicholas   Put the gun down before anybody gets hurt.

William   Don't be fucking stupid.

It feels funny. It's a lot lighter than I thought it would be. It's a lot easier to aim.

Hey, Bennett. Hey, Bennett. Get up. Bennett. Stop fucking crying and fucking listen to me.

You know when you spat at Tanya, what was it like?

What did it feel like?

What was it like for you, Tanya?

Tanya   William, stop it.

William   I heard you got a detention. Shit.

Did your parents find out?

Bennett. Did your parents find out?

Did your parents find out about your detention, Bennett?

Bennett   No.

William   Didn't they?

How come? What did you tell them? What did you tell them, Bennett?

Bennett   I told them I was at football practice.

William   Ha! Did you? How did you think of that? That's fucking brilliant. That's fucking genius is what that is.

Can I tell you something, Bennett?

No other animal in the world polices its behaviour via a third person. Did you know that?

Bennett   Did I know what?

William   If a monkey steals another monkey's nuts he doesn't go and get a third monkey to sort him out. If a cat shits on another cat's tree that cat doesn't go and tell a big huge third cat and get him to sort the first cat out. Does he? No. Of course he doesn't. Only human beings do that. I hate it. You spat at Tanya. Tanya should have stabbed you or something. She didn't. She rang home and told her dad. It's pathetic. As far as I'm concerned that means you're free to do whatever you want with her. Batter her. Shoot her. Rape her. She's the only one who should be able to stop you.

Don't you think?

Don't you think, Bennett?

Everybody's being really fucking quiet today.

Don't you think, Nicholas, shouldn't Bennett be allowed to rape Tanya now?

Nicholas   No.

William   What?

Nicholas   I said no. He shouldn't. That's horrible. That's a crazy idea.

William   What did you say?

He looks at him for a long time.

Nicholas   I said that's a crazy idea.

William   Don't say that.

Nicholas   We can't operate like –

Bennett   Don't, Nicholas.

Nicholas   We can't control a community –

Bennett   Nicholas, be quiet for God's sake.

William   Ah! That's quite sweet. She's protecting you, look.

I don't want to talk about this any more.

He shoots **Bennett** *twice. He dies.* **Cissy** *screams. She tries to stop herself.*

There is some quietness. Some stillness for a while.

William   Can you smell burning?

Something's burning. Can you smell?

Nicholas   No.

William   Here. Nicholas.

Nicholas   What?

William   Watch this.

He shoots **Cissy**. *She dies.*

Nicholas   William!

Tanya *is crying.* **Chadwick** *is crying.*

William   Did you say something?

Chadwick   Me?

William   Yeah.

Chadwick   No.

William   I thought you said something.

Chadwick   I didn't.

William   I thought somebody said something. Just now. About – did you say something about a fire?

Chadwick   No.

William   You did. I heard you.

Chadwick   I didn't, William.

William   It's probably just me. Is it just me? Am I the only one who heard him talking about the fire?

This happens to me all the time.

He points his gun at **Nicholas**.

William   You know when you're thinking?

Nicholas   Thinking? Yes. I know when I'm thinking –

William   When you're thinking, yeah, and in order to like make a decision, yes? Sometimes you have to weigh one side up against the other and you need to have a jolly good debate in your head about what is the right thing to do and what is the wrong thing to do, yes? And sometimes when you're doing this each side kind of has a voice in your head. You know that?

Nicholas   I think so, William.

William   Sometimes when I do that – the voices sound like they're coming from over there. Or over there. Or over there. Sometimes. Not often. That sounded as though it was coming from Chadwick. How very embarrassing. I am sorry.

Nicholas   Don't be.

William   I am. I will be. Because I am. You can't exactly choose these things can you?

Can you hear anybody coming?

They listen.

Told you.

William *turns away from* **Chadwick**. *Without* **William** *noticing* **Chadwick** *takes the opportunity to turn and run through the classroom door.*

William *notices him too late. He points his gun. He puts it down again. He laughs a little.*

He got away!

He turns and shoots **Nicholas**. **Nicholas** *dies.*

He looks around at what he's done.

There's some time. He looks at **Tanya**. *She's crying her heart out.*

William   Did you hear about Lilly?

Tanya   What about her.

William   She's dead.

Tanya   Dead?

William   Not literally. She's just in a bit of trouble.

Tanya   Why?

William   She did something.

Tanya   What?

William   Something really bad.

Tanya   What did she do?

William   What's wrong?

Tanya   Nothing.

William   You're crying.

Tanya   Yeah.

William   You're so lovely. Don't cry. Here.

He smiles. Goes to hug her. She is terrified. He hugs her. Lets go. Sits down on a table.

A long pause.

Dear God. Please – Dear God . . . Are you there? Dear God, please look after little baby Alistair and Mum and Dad and –

He breaks into uncontrollable giggles.

I always find it hard to keep a straight face.

He goes to shoot himself. He holds his gun in his mouth. After a short while he retracts it.

I'm sorry. I really need a piss. Should I do it on the floor? Should I do it in my trousers, Tanya? If I do it in my trousers will you tell?

Tanya   No.

William   Do you think it'd be all right?

She nods.

He pisses in his trousers, down his trouser leg, onto the floor of the common room.

My God. The relief.

He breaks into an enormous smile.

Scene Seven

'Desperate Man Blues' by Daniel Johnston.

It's Wednesday 24 December, 11.59 a.m.

William Carlisle *and* **Dr Richard Harvey** *are in a clinical examination room of Suttons Manor medium security hospital.*

The walls of the room are white. It is very brightly lit.

Dr Harvey *wears an immaculately smart brown suit.* **William** *wears joggers and sweat shirt.*

William *is completing a questionnaire.*

He has to tick boxes in answers to questions.

The questionnaire is twenty-five pages long.

There is some time before **Dr Harvey** *speaks.*

Dr Harvey   Would you like to rest?

William   No.

Dr Harvey   You can do.

William   I don't want to.

He answers another question.

I like this kind of test.

It's quite funny.

Have you done it?

Did you make these questions up?

Dr Harvey   With a colleague.

William   How many are there in total?

Dr Harvey   One thousand eight hundred.

William *looks at him. Smiles.*

William   Great.

It's like doing a comprehension test. A bit.

Doing a comprehension test on your brain.

'Do you feel confident in clothes shops?'

'Do you feel confident in music shops?'

'Do you feel confident in cafés?'

'Do you feel confident in libraries?'

'Do you feel confident in supermarkets?'

'Do you feel confident at football matches?'

'Do you feel confident in school classrooms?'

'Do you feel confident in furniture shops?'

'Do you feel confident in licensed adult shops?' Is that sex shops?

Dr Harvey   That's right.

William   'Do you feel confident in greengrocers?'

'Do you feel confident in newsagents?'

'Do you feel confident in playgrounds?'

'Do you feel confident in estate agents?'

He fills in more of the forms.

Dr Harvey *watches him. He writes a little as he's talking.*

After a while **William** *puts his pen down.*

William   I'm not allowed a cigarette, am I?

Dr Harvey   I'm afraid not.

William   I could just have a cheeky one.

Dr Harvey *smiles.*

William   You laugh but I'm being serious.

I'm getting a bit tired now. You shouldn't have put the idea in my head.

It's the Droperidal. The Holoperidal.

He answers a question. He looks up again.

Is it Christmas yet?

Dr Harvey   Tomorrow.

William   It's Christmas Eve?

Dr Harvey   That's right.

William *thinks.*

William   Do you know who I am?

Dr Harvey   Sorry?

William   I never know with you lot if they tell you who I am before I meet you or if they try and keep it neutral.

Dr Harvey   I'm not sure if I know what you mean.

William   Did they tell you what I did?

That means they did, didn't they?

What's your name?

Dr Harvey   Harvey. Dr Harvey.

William   What's your first name? That's not Harvey too is it? Harvey Harvey? Dr Harvey Harvey?

Dr Harvey   No. My first name's Richard.

William   Happy Christmas, Richard.

Dr Harvey   Happy Christmas.

They smile at each other.

Can I ask you something: when you found out that you were coming to meet me, did you get a bit excited?

Dr Harvey   Excited?

William   It's always exciting meeting celebrities, isn't it?

You must have wondered what I'd be like, did you?

Dr Harvey   I've been doing this job long enough to know that you can never really predict what a patient is going to be like, or how they're going to behave. Regardless of how much of their record you've had access to.

William   Or what you've read about them in newspapers.

Dr Harvey   I honestly don't read newspapers.

William   But you know who I am, don't you? You know what I did? Do you know what I did? Richard, do you know what I did?

Dr Harvey   Yeah. Yes I do.

William   I bet there are a million things you want to ask me, are there?

Actually there are one thousand eight hundred things, eh?

But I bet you want to know more than whether or not I feel confident in estate agents, don't you?

Does it freak you out a bit being in here with me?

Dr Harvey   No.

William   Have you got a panic button?

Dr Harvey   Yes I do.

William   Is it underneath your desk?

Have you got any children? Have you, Richard?

Dr Harvey   I've a daughter.

William   How old is she?

Dr Harvey   She's seventeen.

William   My age.

Does it make you sick what I did?

Does it make you sick what I did?

Dr Harvey   No.

William   You're lying. I can tell by the way you look to the left. When people look to the right they're thinking. When they look to the left they're lying.

Can I have a glass of water, please?

Dr Harvey   Certainly.

He stands to leave.

William   I'll just wait here.

Dr Harvey *enjoys the joke.*

He exits.

Some time.

Nicholas *enters.*

He sits opposite **William.**

William *almost laughs. He stares at him.*

William   Nicholas? Nicky?

He goes to touch his face.

Are you OK? Are you dead?

Does it hurt?

Did I hurt you?

I'm –

William *starts to cry a little bit. He stops himself and rubs his eyes dry furiously.*

Nicholas *stands suddenly.*

He exits as though he'd forgotten something and has to rush to get it.

William *is left on his own.*

He tries to gather himself.

William   Oh fuck.

Dr Harvey *returns with a glass of water and three cigarettes and a box of three matches.*

Dr Harvey   Sorry, the cooler was empty. I had to go up to the second floor.

William   Thank you.

He drinks.

Dr Harvey   I got you these. Here.

He gives **William** *the cigarettes.* **William** *smiles broadly.*

William Fucking hell. Thank you.

He takes a cigarette and opens the matches.

Notices there are only three. Laughs once.

Takes one. Strikes it. Lights his cigarette. Smiles broadly.

That tastes lovely.

He smokes.

See, the main question people have been asking me is why I did it?

Why do people keep asking me that?

Dr Harvey I think people are concerned about you.

William 'Why did you do it, William? What did you do it for? Why did you do that? Why did you do this?'

He answers some more questions. As he answers the questions he talks. His ticking becomes more frantic. By the end of his speech he is almost cutting into the paper with his pen.

Dr Harvey *takes a few notes.*

William I don't know. I don't care. It's a pointless question. It's a stupid question. It's a boring question. Next question please. Next question please. Next question please. Was it because of my mum? No. Was it because of my dad? No. Was it because of my brother? No. Was it because of my school? No. Was it because of the teachers? No. Was it because of Lilly? No. Was it the music I was listening to? No. Was it the films I saw? No. Was it the books that I read? No. Was it the things I saw on the internet? No.

He scribbles onto the paper. Puts his pen down.

I did it because I could. I did it because it felt fucking great.

He smokes.

There was a bullet left in the gun. I was going to shoot myself. I actually put the gun to my mouth. Did you hear about that?

Tanya was there, she could tell you this.

Is she alright? Tanya?

Dr Harvey   She's recovering. She and Chadwick Meade both hope to go back to school at the start of next term.

William *thinks about this.*

William   I needed a piss.

So, I just like, I just did a piss there. In the classroom. On the floor.

It felt fucking amazing. I thought if I died I'd never feel that, that, that relief.

Dr Harvey   That's caused by the release of endorphins in our bloodstreams. There are hormones called endorphins which are released when we urinate. They allow us to feel that sense of euphoria.

William *looks at him for a beat.*

William   When you went to get the water, were you watching me? You don't need to answer that, by the way.

Dr Harvey *smiles.*

William   Will you be coming back after today?

Dr Harvey   We don't know yet. I need to complete my report by the end of next week.

William *nods.*

William   What are you going to say about me in your report?

Dr Harvey   I don't quite know yet.

William   Is that a lie? I bet that's a lie. Are you not allowed to tell me when you do know?

Dr Harvey   I'm sure eventually you'll be able to see it.

William   And after you they'll probably send somebody else.

Dr Harvey   That hasn't been decided.

William   They probably will. They send new people all the time.

He answers another question then looks up again.

It needn't be like this, you know?

Dr Harvey   What?

William   Not everybody feels like I feel.

Some people. They're funny. I like them. They tolerate other people. There are people who tolerate other people. They take the piss out of themselves. They work hard to try to make things better.

You can see some of them. You can see them in Year Seven and they look alright. They're wily. You know?

My dad's lived in Stockport all his life. You can walk from house to house to all the houses he's lived in. It takes about an hour. I've done it. He's going to come and visit me, he said. I'm not entirely sure if he'll know how to get here.

He answers another question.

When I was eight I stole some money from my mum's purse. It was about two pounds. I never even spent it. I just wanted to know what it felt like. I watch porno when nobody's in my house. Loads and loads of it. You can get them on the internet for free really easily. My favourite is when it's lesbians.

Sometimes I didn't do my homework. Sometimes I copied it from – there are websites you can go to. I copied it.

I smoke. I have smoked a lot of things actually. I've drunk alcohol. I inhale Tipp-Ex sometimes.

He answers some more questions. Then stops.

I should go and get a job. Do something proper. Do something worthwhile, I think. Don't you think?

Dr Harvey   In time.

William   No. Not in time. Now.

Look. I'm not an – I'm not. I'm not an idiot. I know that something's going on. I know something's a bit wrong.

I want to be an architect. Build buildings way up as high as I can get them to go. Get some children. Just be normal. Go to hospital one day and get my head sorted out. Buy a small house. Not spend too much money.

He answers some more questions. Then stops.

He looks up. He looks at **Dr Harvey**.

Light falls suddenly.

Methuen Drama Student Editions

Jean Anouilh *Antigone* • John Arden *Serjeant Musgrave's Dance*
Alan Ayckbourn *Confusions* • Aphra Behn *The Rover* • Edward Bond
Lear • *Saved* • Bertolt Brecht *The Caucasian Chalk Circle* • *Fear and
Misery in the Third Reich* • *The Good Person of Szechwan* • *Life of Galileo* •
Mother Courage and her Children • *The Resistible Rise of Arturo Ui* • *The
Threepenny Opera* • Anton Chekhov *The Cherry Orchard* • *The Seagull* •
Three Sisters • *Uncle Vanya* • Caryl Churchill *Serious Money* • *Top Girls*
• Shelagh Delaney *A Taste of Honey* • Euripides *Elektra* • *Medea*•
Dario Fo *Accidental Death of an Anarchist* • Michael Frayn *Copenhagen*
• John Galsworthy *Strife* • Nikolai Gogol *The Government Inspector* •
Robert Holman *Across Oka* • Henrik Ibsen *A Doll's House* • *Ghosts*•
Hedda Gabler • Charlotte Keatley *My Mother Said I Never Should* •
Bernard Kops *Dreams of Anne Frank* • Federico García Lorca *Blood
Wedding* • *Doña Rosita the Spinster* (bilingual edition) •*The House of
Bernarda Alba* • (bilingual edition) • *Yerma* (bilingual edition) • David
Mamet *Glengarry Glen Ross* • *Oleanna* • Patrick Marber *Closer* • John
Marston *Malcontent* • Martin McDonagh *The Lieutenant of Inishmore* •
Joe Orton *Loot* • Luigi Pirandello *Six Characters in Search of an Author*
• Mark Ravenhill *Shopping and F***ing* • Willy Russell *Blood Brothers*
• *Educating Rita* • Sophocles *Antigone* • *Oedipus the King* • Wole
Soyinka *Death and the King's Horseman* • Shelagh Stephenson *The
Memory of Water* • August Strindberg *Miss Julie* • J. M. Synge *The
Playboy of the Western World* • Theatre Workshop *Oh What a Lovely
War* Timberlake Wertenbaker *Our Country's Good* • Arnold Wesker
The Merchant • Oscar Wilde *The Importance of Being Earnest* •
Tennessee Williams *A Streetcar Named Desire* • *The Glass Menagerie*

Methuen Drama Modern Plays

include work by

Edward Albee
Jean Anouilh
John Arden
Margaretta D'Arcy
Peter Barnes
Sebastian Barry
Brendan Behan
Dermot Bolger
Edward Bond
Bertolt Brecht
Howard Brenton
Anthony Burgess
Simon Burke
Jim Cartwright
Caryl Churchill
Noël Coward
Lucinda Coxon
Sarah Daniels
Nick Darke
Nick Dear
Shelagh Delaney
David Edgar
David Eldridge
Dario Fo
Michael Frayn
John Godber
Paul Godfrey
David Greig
John Guare
Peter Handke
David Harrower
Jonathan Harvey
Iain Heggie
Declan Hughes
Terry Johnson
Sarah Kane
Charlotte Keatley
Barrie Keeffe
Howard Korder

Robert Lepage
Doug Lucie
Martin McDonagh
John McGrath
Terrence McNally
David Mamet
Patrick Marber
Arthur Miller
Mtwa, Ngema & Simon
Tom Murphy
Phyllis Nagy
Peter Nichols
Sean O'Brien
Joseph O'Connor
Joe Orton
Louise Page
Joe Penhall
Luigi Pirandello
Stephen Poliakoff
Franca Rame
Mark Ravenhill
Philip Ridley
Reginald Rose
Willy Russell
Jean-Paul Sartre
Sam Shepard
Wole Soyinka
Simon Stephens
Shelagh Stephenson
Peter Straughan
C. P. Taylor
Theatre de Complicite
Theatre Workshop
Sue Townsend
Judy Upton
Timberlake Wertenbaker
Roy Williams
Snoo Wilson
Victoria Wood